SHIGERU BAN

THE SWATCH/OMEGA CAMPUS

SHIGERU BAN

Philip Jodidio

THE SWATCH/OMEGA CAMPUS

PRESTEL

Munich · London · New York

Shigeru Ban on the third-floor terrace
of the Centre Pompidou-Metz,
May 10, 2010.

TABLE OF CONTENTS

TIME, STRUCTURE, AND FUNCTION

Shigeru Ban and the Swatch/Omega Campus

After early encounters with the cutting edge of American architecture in the 1970s, Shigeru Ban forged his own very specific identity, continually challenging the limits and preconceived ideas of what a building should be. Structures made with paper tubes, or for disaster relief, became his trademarks, even as he used more traditional materials like concrete and wood. In Biel/Bienne, the home of the historic watchmaker Omega and the more recent brand Swatch, he won a competition to design large parts of a new campus, by challenging the program and proposing innovative, ecologically sensitive solutions. His three buildings in Bienne are very much in keeping with the ground-breaking image of Swatch, while also respecting the time-honored quality of Omega.

Founded in 1848 in La Chaux-de-Fond, the workshop that became La Generale Watch Co. moved to nearby Biel/Bienne in 1880 under the name Louis Brandt & Fils. Installed first on Route de Boujean in that city, the firm established itself thereafter at 96 Rue Jakob-Stämpfli. The company first produced a movement called the 19-ligne "OMEGA" calibre in 1894. The success of this movement, which by 1900 was being produced at a rate of 600 units per day, was such that the firm later renamed itself Omega Watch Co. By 1903, Omega was the largest manufacturer of finished watches in Switzerland. In 1930, Omega became part of the SSIH (Société Suisse pour l'Industrie Horlogère) group, which also included Tissot and, as of 1932, the Lemania brands.

From timing for the Olympic Games to the first watch (Omega Speedmaster) qualified by NASA in 1965 for all manned space missions, Omega watches and timing equipment set an international standard that made it one of the most recognizable brands in the world. The Omega Speedmaster Professional was the first watch to be worn on the moon: by Buzz Aldrin, an Apollo 11 astronaut, on July 21, 1969. With the film *GoldenEye* (1995), Omega became the watch of James Bond and has been worn in subsequent Bond movies as well. This association of the watch brand with significant events and famous people is a testimony to its accuracy and design.

From the Quartz Crisis to Swatch

Swiss watchmaking underwent a number of difficult periods, but one of the most marked was the so-called "quartz crisis." Quartz clocks and quartz watches use an electronic oscillator regulated by a quartz crystal to keep time. Beginning in the early 1970s, such watches made serious inroads in the world market, at the expense of traditional, mechanical timepieces. Although Omega created a number of quartz watches, including its Marine Chronometer (1974), Chrono Quartz (1976), and Calibre 1620 (1977), Japanese makers, such as Seiko and Citizen, began to overtake the Swiss firms that continued to insist on mechanical watches. One of the most interesting initiatives to counter this rise of Asian watchmakers was the creation of Swatch by two engineers in 1983. The first collection of 12 Swatch models was introduced on March 1, 1983. The idea behind the low-priced, attractive watches was to reconquer the entry level of the market with prices below 50 Swiss francs. This pricing policy was made possible by the extensive use of plastic but, above all, a Swatch had just 51 parts, as opposed to 100 or more for a traditional wristwatch. An aggressive marketing policy and attractive designs allowed the firm to sell millions of watches.

Aerial photo of the Omega campus taken in 1970. Most of these buildings still exist, but the campus was transformed by Shigeru Ban's new additions.

The Lebanese-Swiss entrepreneur Nicolas G. Hayek founded a consulting firm called Hayek Engineering in Zurich in 1963. In 1983, he created SMH (Swiss Corporation for Microelectronics and Watchmaking Industries Ltd.) through the merger of the Swiss watchmakers ASUAG and SSIH, which of course included the Omega brand. In 1985, with a group of Swiss investors, Hayek then acquired a majority shareholding of the merged group. In 1998, the SMH was renamed the Swatch Group. Under the leadership of Nicolas G. Hayek, the Swatch Group acquired several watchmaking companies, including Blancpain (1992) and Breguet S.A. (1999). Following the death of the elder Hayek in 2010, his daughter Nayla Hayek became the Chairman of the Swatch Group, of which her younger brother Nick Hayek Jr. had been CEO since 2003. The Group acquired the New York jewelry and luxury watch firm Harry Winston in 2013. In 2020, the Swatch Group employed 32,000 persons located in 50 countries. The firm has 17 different brands and is the world's largest maker of finished watches. The Swatch Group also includes electronic systems firms, watchmaking schools, and other ventures.

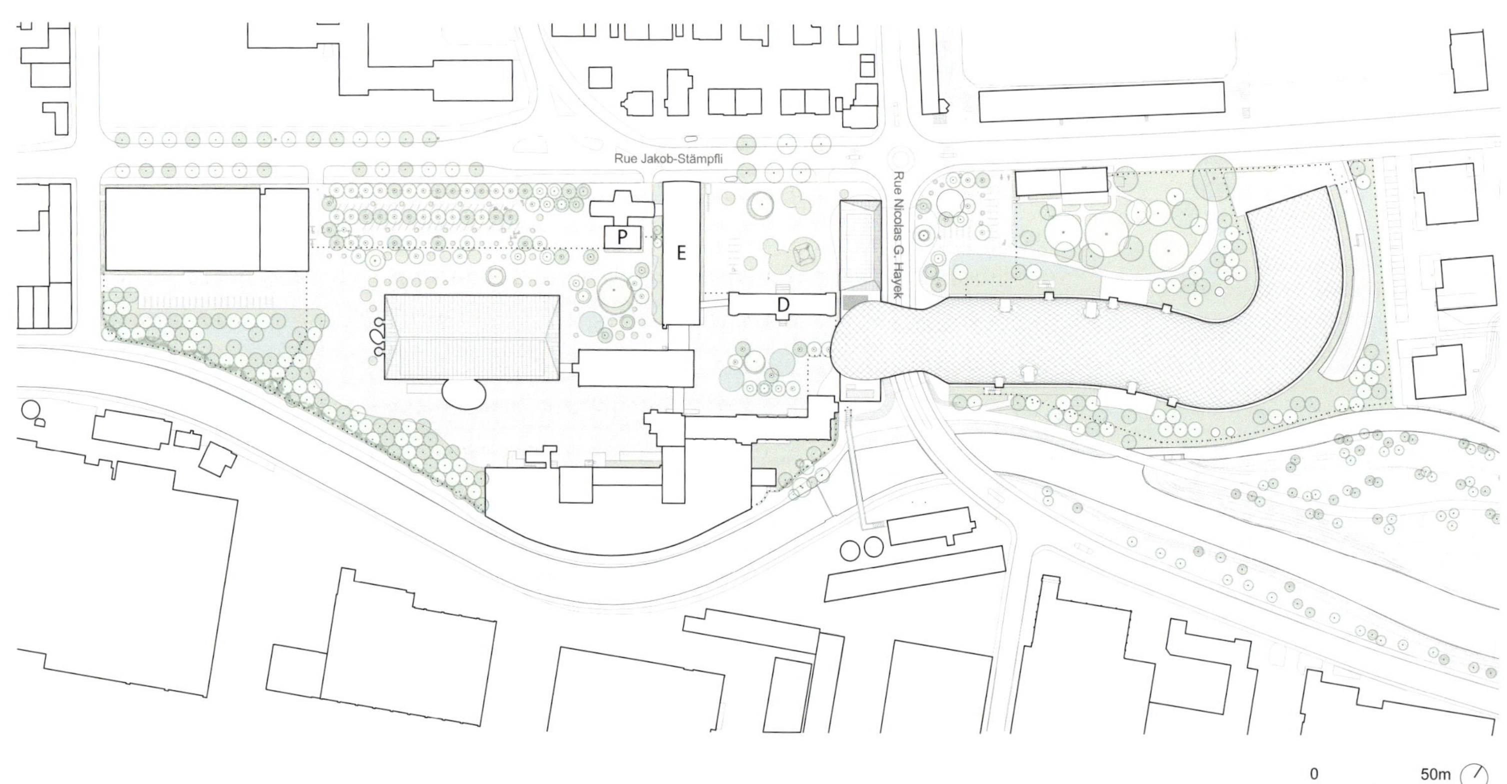

Rue Jakob-Stämpfli
Rue Nicolas G. Hayek
P
E
D
0   50m

Urban Innovation

Over the years, the Omega campus in the bilingual town of Biel/Bienne grew in a largely piecemeal fashion between Rue Jakob-Stämpfli and the Suze river according to the practical needs of the firm. Some buildings of historic interest remained as it became clear that the large Swatch Group and Omega itself needed to modernize the buildings on their trademark site. One of these was the so-called D Building, a watch factory designed and built by the architects Saager & Frey in 1917 near the corner of Rue Jakob-Stämpfli and the former Gottstattstrasse (today's Rue Nicolas G. Hayek). The slender structure in a "neo-baroque" style features a mansard roof and ample glazing for the period, which was intended to bring in as much daylight as possible for the watchmakers. The E building is perpendicular to D and was built in 1953–56 by the Solothurn architect Oskar Sattler. It has a concrete frame and a gridded façade clad in artificial stone and is cited as an "excellent example of Postwar Modernism." It includes a smaller light-metal Porter's House (P building) with a thin flat roof on steel supports, which also still exists.

The Swatch Group launched a competition for several new buildings on and near the Bienne site in 2010. The firm had already planned to install the Swatch Headquarters on a 19,350-square-meter site across the former Gottstattstrasse (now renamed Rue Nicolas G. Hayek) from the original Omega campus which faces Rue Jakob-Stämpfli. The Swatch Group bought the western part of this site from the City of Biel/Bienne, subsequent to a public vote approval concerning the overall urban planning of the district, at the end of November 2008. Called the Gygax area, the site was formerly occupied by the Wyss garden center. As of 2008, the overall site was split into three areas today respectively owned by the Swatch Group, the City of Biel/Bienne, and Previs (the pension fund of the Bernese municipalities). A housing complex was built on the Previs land and a new park was created to the south near the Suze river (Schüssinsel) by the city. The resolution of the land issues posed by the Gygax area was an exemplary case of fruitful collaboration between private (Swatch), public (City of Biel/Bienne), and quasi-governmental organizations (Previs). The competition brief suggested three separate buildings (administration, research, and storage) for the Swatch Headquarters and set aside rectangular blocks in front of the D building for a brand museum and conference building on Rue Jakob-Stämpfli, and at the western side of the site, for a new Omega Factory.

The Swatch Group launched a competition for several new buildings for the Bienne site in 2010.

Top: a bird's eye view of the Swatch Headquarters and Cité du Temps from the east. The large chimneys visible next to the building are air inlet/outlets. The beige footpath is a hiking trail.

Left: a site plan shows the original Omega site to the left, and the newly purchased plot to the right where the Swatch Headquarters was built.

The Swatch Group has released little information about the actual competition, but it is known that there were eight invited participants. Design proposals by other architects were not disclosed, except in cases where the architects have put their proposals on their own web sites. The competition brief requested few connections between the new buildings and the existing campus and imagined a Swatch Headquarters not physically related to the opposite side of the street and the area of the Omega buildings. It was requested that structures for Omega and Swatch be differentiated to reflect the characters of the brands. Shigeru Ban took surprising decisions, first by imagining the Swatch Headquarters as a curving wooden grid shell covered partly with ETFE and partly with glass, and then by proposing to have the Swatch Headquarters roof cross over today's Rue Nicolas G. Hayek, covering a conference center at the top of the new Cité du Temps brand museum and event building. Lifted up on *pilotis* and placed parallel to the street instead of directly in front of the D building, the Cité du Temps, together with the D and E structures, forms a U-shaped square now aptly named Omega Plaza, opening toward Rue Jakob-Stämpfli. With automobile traffic on the street between the Swatch Headquarters and the Omega campus limited to 30 kilometers per hour, it became possible for pedestrians to cross directly over, passing under the Cité du Temps to Omega Plaza. Using wood structures for most of the three new buildings (including the Omega Factory further to the west), Shigeru Ban proposed not only practical solutions to the Swatch Group requests, but actually improved on them while giving the entire dual campus a forward-looking and modern appeal. Shigeru Ban's proposal was coupled with a gentle tree-filled grid landscaping solution imagined by the Basel firm Fontana Landschaftarchitektur. Tying together the Swatch/Omega campuses and the city in the Gygax area, Fontana was also responsible for the neighboring Schüssinsel Park (2010–15) along the banks of the Suze.

Strict Rules and Limited Materials

The background of Shigeru Ban is unusual, beginning with his choices for the study of architecture. Born in 1957 in Tokyo, he attended the Southern California Institute of Architecture (SCI-Arc, 1977–80), and then the Cooper Union in New York. He returned to Japan and worked in the office of Arata Isozaki (1982–83) before coming back to the Cooper Union (1983–84), where he studied under Peter Eisenman, and worked on his diploma project with John Hejduk. Shigeru Ban founded his own firm in Tokyo in 1985. Few noted Japanese architects at the time, with the exception of figures like Fumihiko Maki or Yoshio Taniguchi, had studied outside of Japan, but his departure from more usual patterns began even earlier. "At first," says Ban, "I wanted to be a carpenter. My parents extended their house on several occasions, so it seemed that there was always a carpenter working in the house. As a child, I would pick up the small leftover pieces of wood to make something out of them, like a model train or a building. Perhaps it has to do with the education my parents gave me, but I hate to throw things away. I guess then that I have a natural predisposition to reuse things." Again explaining his early motivations and formative experiences, he says: "To enter the Japanese art school, we had to create a tower higher than one meter just using cardboard, and without wasting materials. Working with strict rules and a limited amount of materials was something I was very good at. I saw my teacher again a few years ago, and he said to me, 'You are still doing the same things.'"[1]

"When I was in high school," continues the architect, "I was interested in going to art school to study architecture. It was necessary to do a lot of drawings or to make models. One of the best art schools in Japan had a school of architecture and I wanted to go there. I went to a kind of prep school for this type of study and my teacher there was an architect. It was with him in 1975 that I saw a special issue of the magazine *A+U* on the architect John Hejduk. I saw that he taught at the Cooper Union in New York. At the time, there was no Internet and nobody really knew much about Cooper Union in Japan. I had to go to the US and I did not speak any English. I did see in a brochure that they did not accept foreign students unless they transferred from another US institution. So I looked for another school of architecture in the US that would admit me so that I could then transfer to Cooper Union. It could have been any school but, with some luck, I selected SCI-Arc in California. I applied there in 1977 and the school had been established in 1974, so it was really new. Eric Owen Moss, Thom Mayne, and Frank Gehry were all involved in it. I was fortunate enough to have an interview with the school's founder Ray Kappe. He liked my portfolio and I was admitted into the second year, even before I had passed an English exam. SCI-Arc was more interesting than I expected, so I stayed there two and a half years. I still wanted to go to Cooper Union though, so I was admitted there in the second year, which means I lost the credits I had earned at SCI-Arc. Nonetheless, I managed to do the third- and fourth-year programs in New York in a single year."

Following double page:
a site rendering shows the three new structures on the site, each with a different design language to represent the characters of the brands and the use of the buildings.

Omega Factory

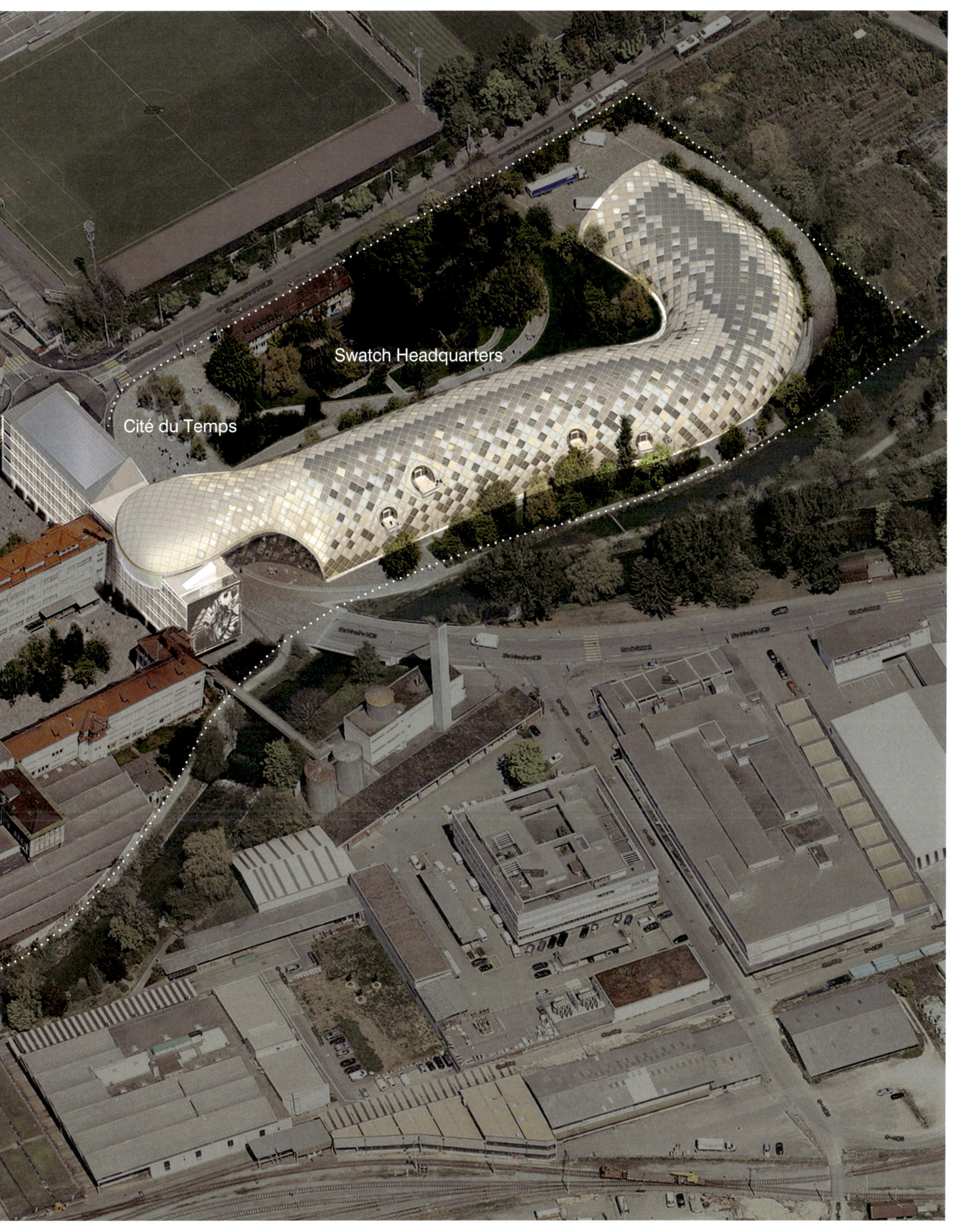

Swatch Headquarters
Cité du Temps

Cardboard tower designs conceived by Shigeru Ban when he was attending an art school in Japan, before his studies in the United States.

From Wall to Wall-less

Shigeru Ban carried indirect influences both from his California experience and from his time studying under John Hejduk in New York. He named many of his residential projects Case Study Houses, in keeping with the celebrated program of contemporary houses sponsored by *Arts & Architecture* magazine between 1945 and 1966 in southern California. That work, designed by architects such as Richard Neutra, Charles and Ray Eames, Craig Ellwood, Pierre Koenig, Eero Saarinen, and others, challenged even the basic ideas of house design. Shigeru Ban, too, sought systematically to ask if the conventions of residential architecture could be called on to evolve substantially. Hejduk, perhaps better known as a "paper architect" than as an active builder, experimented with grids and frames, proposing such iconic works as Wall House 2. Designed in 1973 for a site in Ridgefield, Connecticut, and finally built, after Hejduk's death, in the Netherlands, Wall House 2 was based, as its name implies, on a very

16

From the likes
of John Hejduk,
Shigeru Ban
carried forward
and developed an
intellectual approach
to architecture.

large concrete wall with stacked, curving elements attached on one side. It is not a coincidence that Shigeru Ban later designed the Wall-less House (Nagano, Japan, 1997). He, too, sought to ask fundamental questions about what constitutes a house, or, more broadly, how architecture can respond to a given question. From the likes of Hejduk, Shigeru Ban carried forward and developed not any stylistic imitation but, instead, an intellectual approach to architecture.

Though he attributes his good fortune in attending SCI-Arc in its early years to coincidence, the young man thus found himself in the company of some of the most creative and significant American architects of the time. Gehry was at the height of his inventiveness in the 1970s as was the future Pritzker winner Thom Mayne of Morphosis. Shigeru Ban's journey to the classroom of John Hejduk was clearly willful. Indeed, he has shown a propensity for gravitating toward exceptional, creative figures, including architects and engineers, throughout his career. Without imitating any of them, he seems to have drawn much of his own vital force from them.

Practical and Inspirational

Shigeru Ban came to broad international attention with works such as the Metal Shutter House on West 19th Street in New York (USA, 2010), the Centre Pompidou-Metz (Metz, France, 2010; see p.38), Aspen Art Museum (Colorado, USA, 2014), Oita Prefectural Art Museum (Oita, Japan, 2015), and La Seine Musicale (Île Seguin, Boulogne-Billancourt, France, 2017; see p.42). His recent work in Switzerland, including the Tamedia Headquarters in Zurich (see p.41) and, of course, the Swatch/Omega campus in Bienne, affirms his continuing presence as a seasoned international master of architecture. Shigeru Ban does refer to some extent to Japanese tradition when that is germane, but he is, above all, an architect who seeks to push back the limits of his art, combining structure and design in a seamless, surprising, yet thoroughly logical whole. In granting him the 2014 Pritzker Prize, Lord Palumbo, Chairman of the Jury said: "At Bienne in Switzerland, Ban has made a headquarters for the Swatch company and a production factory building for Omega. His astonishing light-filled structure uses engineered wood to express simultaneous passions for renewable materials and precision. So Shigeru Ban can be practical and inspirational simultaneously. He is simply a great architect as well as a beacon of life pointing the way forward for others in his profession to make this all for the best in this best of possible worlds. His simplicity is rare, precious, and inspirational. This is Shigeru Ban on hearing the news of this year's award: 'Receiving this prize is a great honor,' he said, 'and with it I must be careful. I must continue to listen to the people I work for in my private commissions and in my disaster-relief work. I see you, the prize, as encouragement for me to keep doing what I am doing, not to change what I am doing, but to grow.' His fellow architect Lee Mindel pays tribute to him in 15 words: 'Shigeru Ban,' he says, 'is the conscience of our generation of architects, manifest in the built form.' What a fitting epitaph those words would make. No one could ask for more. For this and for the other reasons that I attempted to identify, we're proud to honor Shigeru Ban today as laureate of the 2014 Pritzker Prize for Architecture."[2]

Working often with paper tubes and engineered wood, as is the case in Bienne, Shigeru Ban is cited as an exemplary "green" architect, yet, as he points out, this is not really his intention. "I am often thought of as an 'eco-designer,'" says Ban, "yet when I started working with recycled materials in 1986, no one was talking about 'ecology' and 'sustainability.' Now those words are a fad and a commercial consumer product. I don't use recycled materials because it's fashionable, but because I don't want to waste them. When *The New York Times* critic Michael Kimmelman heard my story, he gave me a new title: 'The Accidental Environmentalist.'" Kimmelman also wrote: "His works are airy, curvaceous, balletic. An heir to Buckminster Fuller and Oscar Niemeyer, to Japanese traditional architecture and to Alvar Aalto, he is an old-school Modernist with a poet's touch and an engineer's inventiveness."[3]

1. Shigeru Ban in conversation with the author, Paris, December 9, 2008.

2. Lord Palumbo, at https://www.pritzkerprize.com/2014/ceremony-speech-0, accessed January 10, 2021.

3. Michael Kimmelman, "The Accidental Environmentalist," *The New York Times Magazine*, May 20, 2007, at https://www.nytimes.com/2007/05/20/magazine/20shigeru-t.html, accessed January 10, 2021.

Shigeru Ban delivering his acceptance speech for the Pritzker Prize, Rijksmuseum, Amsterdam, June 13, 2014. To the left of the architect in this image, Martha Thorne (Executive Director of the Prize), Eberhard van der Laan (Mayor of Amsterdam), Peter Palumbo, and Thomas J. Pritzker.

I AM A FORM-FINDER NOT A FORM-GIVER

Shigeru Ban in conversation
with the author

As he explains his approach, Shigeru Ban makes clear that he
is far from seeking any formatted style, preferring, instead,
to continually challenge the assumptions of contemporary
architecture and, at the same time, to expand his own horizons.
Fascinated by the ideas born of collaboration, he has turned
to the German architect Frei Otto, but also to people like the
Swiss wood engineer Hermann Blumer. And yet it is also clear
that Ban's idea of collaboration is often aimed at developing and
carrying out his own concept of an architectural project. It is in
this sense that he is a form-finder and not a form-giver.

You have made frequent use of paper tubes and wood in your architecture. When did you start actively thinking about those materials?

Shigeru Ban Beginning in 1985, I organized three exhibitions at the Axis Gallery in Tokyo. The first of these was dedicated to Emilio Ambasz. I was interested in Ambasz because he was a graphic and industrial designer as well as an architect. I was also interested in his way of presenting things—there was always a very functional idea behind his projects.

For this first exhibition at the Axis Gallery, I used a special fabric to make spaces. When we had finished hanging the fabric, only the paper tubes remained. Instead of throwing them away, I brought them back to my office.

And what did you do with those paper tubes?

SB My second exhibition design for the Axis Gallery concerned work by Alvar Aalto. I must admit that I was not at all interested in Aalto when I was a student. My first job when I graduated from the Cooper Union was working for the architectural photographer Yukio Futagawa as his assistant. He took me to Finland, and I can say that I was really "shocked" by the discovery of the work of Aalto. I knew from my studies what to expect when I went to visit buildings by Le Corbusier or Mies van der Rohe, but when I saw the work of Alvar Aalto, it was somehow different. His work can only really be experienced when you visit his buildings. His buildings depend on the context, climate, or the different texture of the materials. Since then, I became a great fan of Alvar Aalto, and in 1986 I decided to move his exhibition of furniture and glass from the Museum of Modern Art[1] to the Axis Gallery (see p.34). They had a limited budget, but I also hated the idea of using a precious material such as wood for a temporary exhibition. I looked for some alternative material to replace wood for the partitions or ceilings and I thought that maybe the paper tubes I had saved from the Ambasz show could be the right solution. I used them as a kind of recycled structural material, so my work in exhibition organization had a very great influence on my career.[2]

Was your decision to use paper tubes related to ecological concerns?

SB Concern for the environment was not the main reason for my development. I am aware that because the environmental movement has become more present in recent years, what I do has a new power to convince clients. For me, paper tubes were above all a very inexpensive construction material. When I started to work on disaster-relief projects, with recycled paper that is available cheaply anywhere in the world, that has another meaning. There is no ecological intention in the development of my work.

For your Japanese Pavilion at Expo 2000 (Hanover, Germany, 2000; see p.35) you used a grid-shell design made with paper tubes. Was that the first time you created such a shell?

SB It was the first time I used a grid-shell structure, and, above all, I worked with Frei Otto. I was a fan of Frei Otto when I was at SCI-Arc. I also dreamed of designing Expo structures. When I got the commission to design the Japanese Pavilion at the Hanover Expo 2000 exhibition, I immediately thought that I needed a local, strong architect or engineer to help me.

For the Centre Pompidou-Metz in France in 2010 (see p.38), you again employed a kind of shell structure, but this time in wood.

SB It was the first time I collaborated with the Swiss wood engineer Hermann Blumer. For my own development as an architect, it was very important to collaborate with masters such as Frei Otto and Hermann Blumer. When I entered the Metz competition, I collaborated with Cecil Balmond to whom I had been introduced by Arata Isozaki, but we had totally different attitudes toward structure. When we won the competition, we had to work with another engineering team from Ove Arup with whom I also had disagreements. This project was finally built as I originally designed it, but Arup did not accept my ideas and their concept would have cost twice the allowed budget. I was sure that my original design could be built cheaply. At that time, I met with the wood engineer Hermann Blumer and he agreed that we could realize my design within the budget.

Shigeru Ban designed the 1986 exhibition of the work of Alvar Aalto at the Axis Gallery in Tokyo.

Did your use of wood in Metz in 2010 have any ecological reasoning behind it?

SB I am interested in using "weak" materials. I like to use materials that have limitations. Steel is mighty, you can make anything you want. Paper tubes and timber have very strict limitations because they are natural materials and also because of the production capacity limitations that exist for paper tubes. What I want is to use these limitations in my designs. I understood from the beginning that the durability and the strength of the structure has nothing to do with the strength of the material itself. A concrete structure can easily be destroyed by an earthquake whereas a building made with paper tubes or timber may be able to resist better. I always thought of paper-tube structures as potentially being very durable. When I was a student I was very interested in Frei Otto and in Buckminster Fuller because they are the two architects who were not interested in the fashionable styles of their time. They both developed structural systems and their materials.

Both the Hanover Pavilion and the Centre Pompidou-Metz are characterized by ample, curving roofs. When you designed the Haesley Nine Bridges Golf Clubhouse (Yeoju, South Korea, 2010; see p.40), you opted for an essentially flat, wooden roof system. Why is that?

SB For the Golf Club there was no reason to make a curved roof. In the case of the Centre Pompidou-Metz, the reason was the condition underneath, which includes three tube-shaped galleries, and also the need for appropriate drainage. The shape of the roofs is not arbitrary or subjective; on the contrary, it is very efficient given the structure below.

Why did you choose to use wood for the Tamedia building (Zurich, Switzerland, 2011–13; see p.41)?

SB I am interested in using wood in any building. If I were to use steel, it would be very difficult for me to find the best solution. Steel offers a great deal of freedom of design. If I have a huge site and no budgetary limitations, I don't know what to do. I intentionally try to limit myself so that I can find the design concept. Using wood is a way to limit myself.

What other advantages do you see to using wood, and what about cost levels? Do you relate your use of wood to your Japanese origins?

SB The cost of a comparable building in steel or concrete is similar. Using the latest technologies, a wood structure can be more precise than a building made with steel or concrete. Switzerland and Germany are two countries that have very advanced timber technology. Traditional carpentry in Japan, on the other hand, is perhaps the best in the world. After the War, the government discouraged the use of timber.

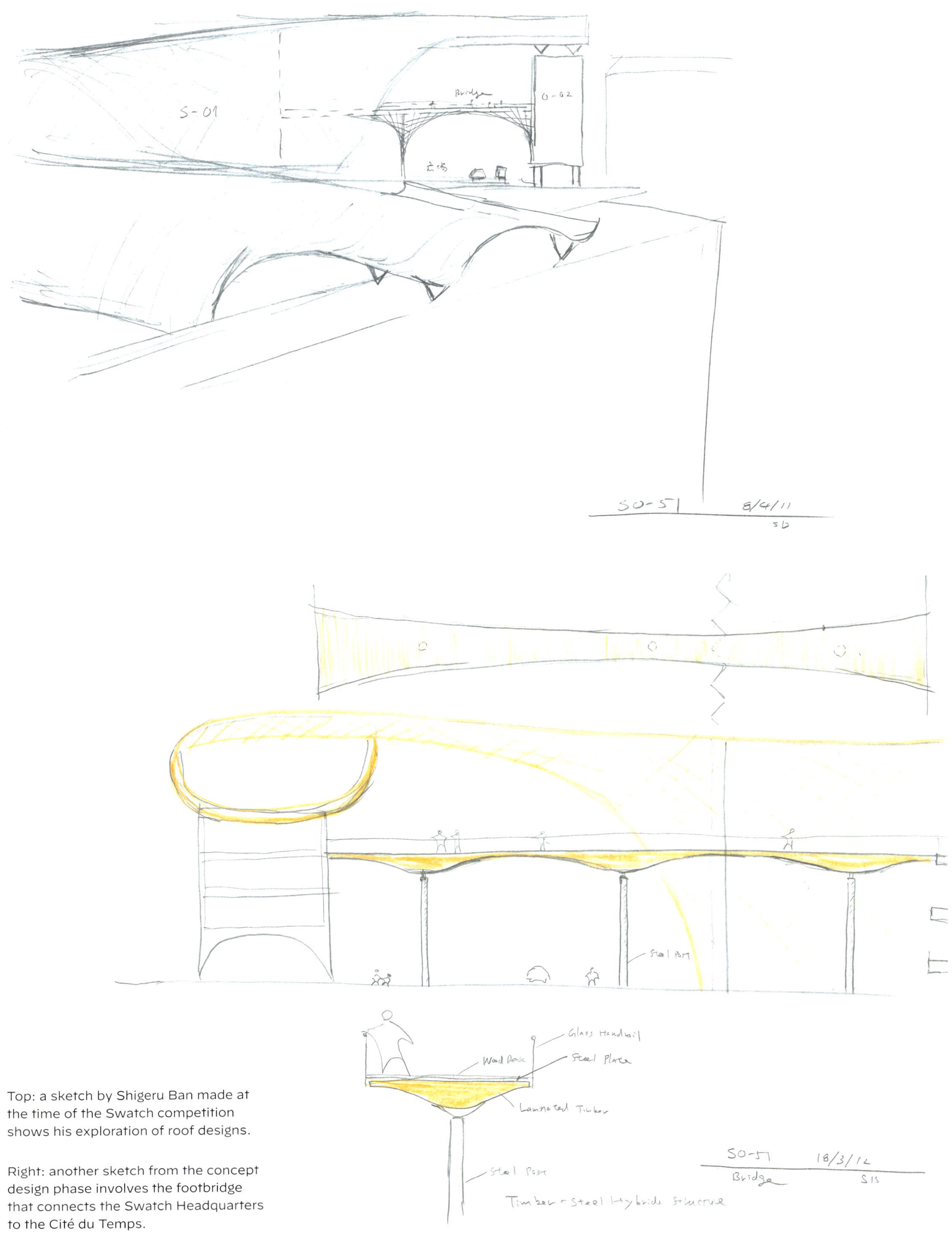

Top: a sketch by Shigeru Ban made at the time of the Swatch competition shows his exploration of roof designs.

Right: another sketch from the concept design phase involves the footbridge that connects the Swatch Headquarters to the Cité du Temps.

SWATCH
SWISS
TIME IS WHAT YOU MAKE OF IT

DON'T
STOP
ME!

swatch

TACHYMÈTRE
OMEGA
Speedmaster
PROFESSIONAL

MASTER
CHRONOMETER
CO - AXIAL
OMEGA
3861
THE FIRST WATCH
WORN ON THE MOON
Stainless Steel
OMEGA

Timber engineering was not developed as a result of this policy.

For a building like Tamedia, you say that you do not use wood for ecological reasons, but it is nonetheless an ecologically aware building, is it not?

SB Yes, I do admit to employing ecological reasoning to convince my clients to use wood. This is not the main purpose of my design, but I take advantage of the movement.

For the Seine Musicale (Boulogne-Billancourt, France, 2017; see p.42), you used wood, but only for part of the design. The very visible dome has transparent skin that is supported by a reticulated geometric wood structure; why is that?

SB Here, the building itself could not be built in timber, but the visible structure is in wood for the dome. With a steel building, you need cladding, but not with a timber structure. We don't need to worry about condensation and the connections can be very simple. I always want to make the structure visible. I don't want to criticize other architects but just imagine a building that becomes beautiful because of its cladding, but not because of its structure. Architects like Renzo Piano and Norman Foster often want to design a beautiful structure that is not hidden by cladding. Using computer-driven technology, it is possible to make any shape, then you just cover up the structure with cladding. But I don't find that a fully clad structure is honest. I like honest buildings.

How did you decide to create the very large curving roof of the Swatch Headquarters?

SB For the Swatch site there were many restrictions for the height and the setbacks. The form of the roof comes from those requirements and site conditions—It follows the shape of the site. I am not a form-making architect but, instead, a form-finding architect, which can also be said of Frei Otto.

Although the original campus imagined separate buildings, you created a number of connections; how did you do that?

SB I knew that in Switzerland it is possible to cover a public street under certain conditions, as long as the street remains open to the public. We knew from the program that we had to design the conference hall on top of the second building across the street, which is called the Cité du Temps. Instead of designing a separate roof, I just extended the roof of the Swatch building. One of the program requirements from the client for the competition was that we needed to have completely different identities for Swatch and Omega. For me, playfulness and color are characteristics of Swatch. Omega is more traditional and rigorous. My idea was to show the characteristics of the two companies through the shape of their buildings.

Top: Swatch watches with plastic cases make frequent use of color. They are designed to high-quality standards while remaining affordable and robust.

Left: Omega Speedmaster watches: "The first watch worn on the moon."

Across Rue Nicolas G. Hayek from the Swatch Headquarters, you lifted the Cité du Temps off the ground with *pilotis* to allow people to move through freely, is that not correct?

> **SB** Instead of designing the three buildings separately, I did want to create connections and a unification of the whole campus. The client had originally imagined two different campuses. Administration, research, and storage blocks were planned for Swatch in the client's documents.

There is a square next to the Cité du Temps where the client wanted to build facing Rue Jakob-Stämplfi; why did you leave it empty?

> **SB** The master plan suggested building there, but I didn't want to hide the existing traditional Omega building. The plaza I created faces three buildings. The entire project was conceived simultaneously but built in three phases.

The Cité du Temps and the Omega Factory both use wood, but have different structural characteristics, why is that?

> **SB** The Omega Factory has a large concrete core for the automated sorting system that I surrounded with a timber structure. Because of the concrete core, the post-and-beam connections of the wood did not have to be as rigid. The lateral forces are taken care of by the concrete core. The Cité du Temps does not have a concrete core, and that is why the connection of timber beams and columns must be rigid. This explains the basic structural differences between the Omega Factory and the Cité du Temps. Even the elevator core of the Cité du Temps is a CLT (cross-laminated timber) sheer wall. The wooden structure was specifically designed for this project.

Did fire resistance pose a structure for the wooden designs?

> **SB** According to existing Swiss law, we used what is called oversizing, which is to say extra thickness for the structural elements in wood. A half-hour of extra fire protection is obtained with an extra 25 millimeters of thickness, and 45 millimeters provides one hour of fire protection.

The new structures are environmentally efficient, is that not true?

> **SB** Yes, but environmental issues were once again not my real starting point. The total amount of CO_2 created by a timber structure is about one third of that of a steel structure, and one half of concrete. Clearly, concrete and steel consume resources, whereas wood is a totally renewable construction material. Different types of wood were used depending on the required strength. The main wood was local spruce, with beech hardwood and white ash. The wood is 100% Swiss.

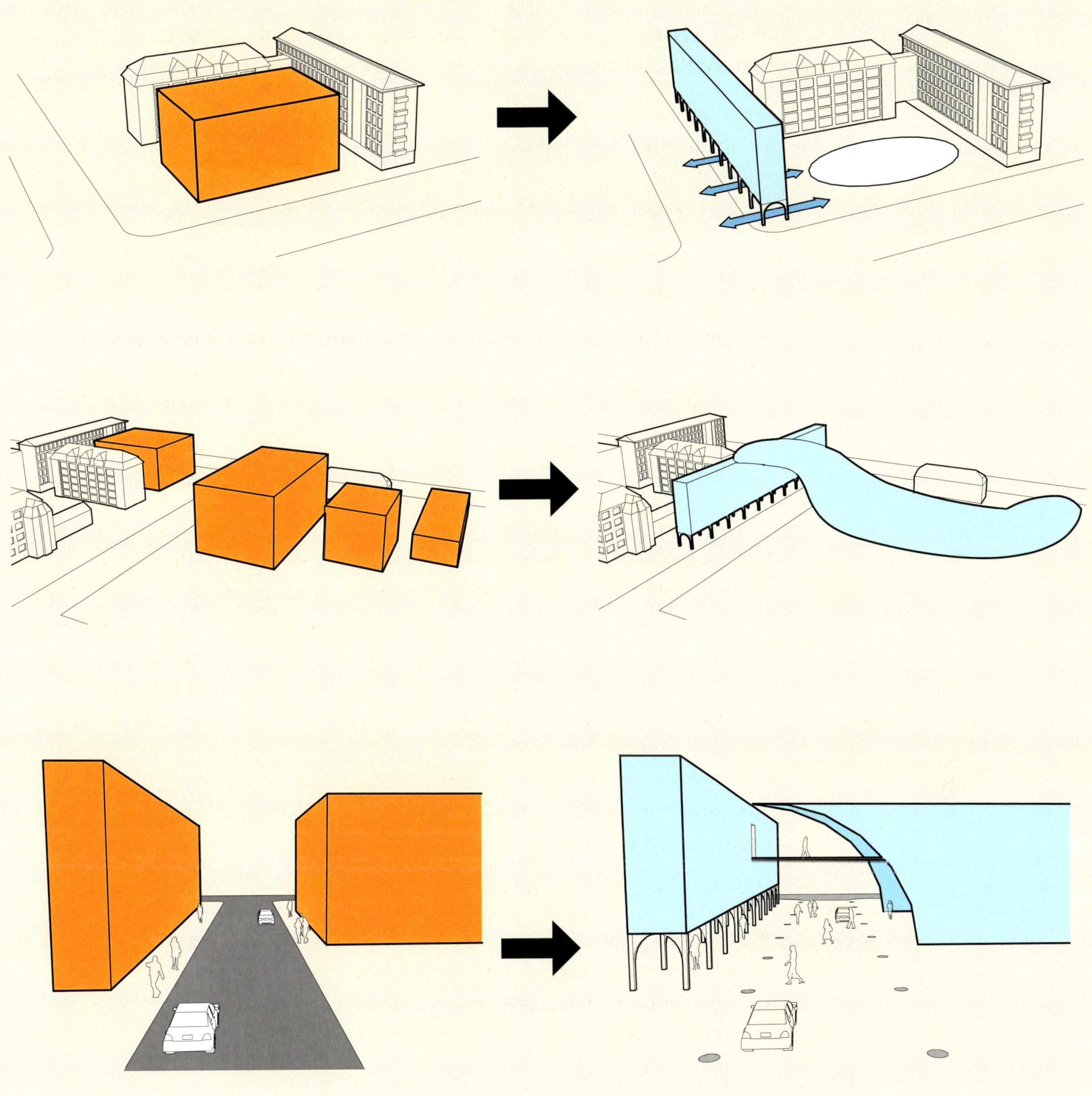

Drawings compare the original
competition program requirements
for the new buildings—colored here in
orange to the scheme of Shigeru Ban (in
blue). Instead of three buildings, Shigeru
Ban proposed a single structure for the
Swatch Headquarters, which he linked
to the Cité du Temps across the street.
By rotating the Cité du Temps, he also
created a new public plaza.

On the western side of the Omega Factory there is a spiral staircase and two unusual cone-shaped forms; what is the reason for that?

> **SB** The air-conditioning machinery is on the roof and the torch or cone-shaped elements also serve as ducts. It is an unusual shape, but it is in relation to the necessary duct sizes. It has to be bigger close to the machines, becoming smaller and smaller as it descends. The spiral staircase is a required fire-escape route. The forms are actually related to engineering calculations and we decided to clad them in stainless steel.

The Omega Factory has large glass surfaces. Is that in part due to the need that watchmakers have for natural light?

> **SB** Yes. It is also restful for the watchmakers to see the greenery outside.

Why is the Omega Factory oriented along the east-west, perpendicular to the Cité du Temps?

> **SB** This is the only building that I placed exactly as the client originally planned. The client needed parking space on the street side, so this orientation made sense.

Do you feel that the quality of construction was what you hoped for?

> **SB** Yes. I must point out that we had a very good client. They did not hire a general contractor. There was a single project manager for all three buildings. The project manager, who works for Hayek Engineering, was also involved in the Hayek Center in Ginza (Tokyo; see p.37), which we designed in 2005. We started by contracting the Omega Factory, but we had to change the concrete subcontractor. We were allowed to select the subcontractors in collaboration with the project manager. The Chairman of the Swatch Group, Nayla Hayek, and her brother Nick Hayek Jr., the CEO of the Group, were directly involved and gave us all of the required approvals for materials and even colors. Some choices were changed according to their requirements.

Was the cost of construction in line with what was requested?

> **SB** The construction was more expensive than they expected, but the project manager controlled the budget and sometimes we had to opt for our second choices.

The Swatch/Omega project took eight and a half years (including the competition) to complete, which seems to be quite a long period; why is that?

1. *Alvar Aalto: Furniture and Glass*, Museum of Modern Art, New York, September 26 – November 27, 1984.

2. Shigeru Ban in conversation with the author, Paris, December 9, 2008. The rest of this text is based on another conversation between the architect and the author, November 16, 2020.

SB A larger general contractor could have built everything at the same time, but Hayek Engineering had a capacity to do them one by one. The first structure was the Omega Factory. Actually, the Cité du Temps and the Swatch Headquarters did wind up advancing more or less simultaneously.

The official ribbon-cutting ceremony for the new Swatch/Omega Campus in Bienne, October 3, 2019. From left to right, Shigeru Ban, Nayla Hayek, and Nick Hayek.

SEVEN KEY PROJECTS

For this book, Shigeru Ban selected seven key projects that bear some relation to the work he did for the Swatch/Omega campus. His choice has to do with the use of wood in earlier projects, but also with his relation to important figures in his career, such as the German architect Frei Otto, the Swiss wood engineer Hermann Blumer, or the client for the projects in Biel/Bienne, the Hayek family. As he insists, each project requires different solutions uniquely related to site and program. Each of these seven projects is clearly different from the architect's work on the historic site of Omega, but they all have some bearing on the solutions and methods he has employed here.

Alvar Aalto Exhibition
Axis Gallery, Tokyo, Japan

In 1985, Shigeru Ban organized the first of three exhibitions on the work of the Argentine-American architect and designer Emilio Ambasz. Made to be easily transported, the show at the Axis Gallery in Tokyo, which went on to the Museum of Contemporary Art in La Jolla, was based on square-section paper tubes framing display units made with flat-folding honeycomb screens. Paper tubes were also used as legs for model stands. The round paper tubes, originally provided with rolls of fabric for the exhibition, were to inspire the architect even more, however. A second exhibition design by Shigeru Ban, in 1986 also at the Axis Gallery, was based on *Alvar Aalto: Furniture and Glass* seen at the Museum of Modern Art in New York from September 26 to November 27, 1984. The architect wanted to "design the exhibition space as an Aalto-like interior," but a limited budget and the temporary nature of the installation dictated that wood, one of Aalto's favored materials, could not be used. Referring back to his experience with the Ambasz show, Ban determined that tubes made of recycled paper could be used to create ceilings, partitions, and display stands for the

220-square-meter show. As well as evoking the undulating lines of Aalto's wood, this use of paper was significant for Shigeru Ban's career. As he says quite simply: "This was the beginning of paper architecture." Shigeru Ban participated in another Aalto exhibition at London's Barbican Art Gallery (*Alvar Aalto Through the Eyes of Shigeru Ban*, February 22–May 13, 2007), evidence of an ongoing interest in the Finnish architect. As Ban says: "I admire the works of Alvar Aalto, whose architecture was modern yet regional, and made much use of natural materials and organic curves."

Although the architect insists that ecological concerns were not his priority, tubes made of recycled paper were clearly not wasteful, and at the same time they were inexpensive and flexible in terms of their use. After the Aalto exhibition, Shigeru Ban began to imagine using paper as an actual structural material. He says: "I was amazed by the strength and precision and variety of the material. My first paper building was a small pavilion for an exhibition in Nagoya (Paper Arbor, Paper Tube Structure 01, Nagoya, Japan, 1989)."

1999 **Japanese Pavilion**
2000 Expo 2000, Hanover, Germany

Shigeru Ban was selected to design the Japanese Pavilion at Expo 2000, one of whose themes was sustainability. As a result, between July 1997 and August 1999, he imagined "a three-dimensional, curved, grid-shell, tunnel arch composed of paper tubes connected with fabric tape and reinforced with wooden ladder arches." A paper membrane developed in Japan and made of five fireproof, water-resistant layers was used for the roof covering. With a total floor area of 3,015 square meters and a height of 16 meters, this was the largest of Shigeru Ban's paper-tube structures. The choice of this paper was particularly apt for Expo 2000 not only because of its environmental emphasis, but also because this pavilion had to reflect some aspect of Japanese tradition. The use of paper also facilitated the demolition and recycling of construction materials. The wave-like form of the building made of 440 cardboard rolls measuring 12 centimeters in diameter and up to 40 meters in length presented engineering challenges. For this project, Shigeru Ban teamed up with the noted German architect Frei Otto, a figure he had long admired. Much of Frei Otto's work sought to achieve the lightest or most economical solution to a given structural problem, whence his abiding interest in natural forms. His German Pavilion for Montreal's Expo 67 (with Rolf Gutbrod) was a 7,730-square-meter PVC-coated polyester fabric structure that took only six weeks to build. Otto went on to design the roof for the Olympic Stadium in Munich (1972). The UK engineers Buro Happold and the largest paper-tube manufacturer in the region also came together to assist Shigeru Ban. Ban concludes: "Supported by its many collaborators, the 'Paper Pavilion' is the successful result of multinational collaboration, as well as of the combination of ideas and technologies." With this high-profile project, Shigeru Ban demonstrated his ability to use an unusual building material in an equally unexpected structural form. He also brought together a reference to Japanese tradition (paper in architecture) with a very contemporary sense of design, in the context of a collaboration with one of the most noted German architects of the period.

2005
2007

Nicolas G. Hayek Center
Ginza, Tokyo, Japan

Named for the founder of the Swatch Group, this narrow 14-story building is located in the Ginza shopping area, where other noted architects, such as Renzo Piano (Maison Hermès, 2001), have worked. This steel-and-reinforced-concrete building has a floor area of 5,697 square meters; it was designed between February and October 2005 and includes areas for the six watch brands of the Swatch Group. A vegetal wall was created on the northeast wall of the atrium, where large glass "showroom" elevators individually serve each of the brand spaces. The green wall is again found on the same wall in the upper-level spaces. This tactic permits the rather narrow building to overcome the necessary stacking of the brand spaces, attracting visitors into the ground floor and drawing them upward. Although wood and paper were not main materials for the Ginza building, Shigeru Ban developed another of his favorite themes in the Center, which features four-story-high glass shutters on both the front and back façades. These open to create a public passageway through the building, and a certain ambiguity between interior and exterior areas, an element that is frequent in Japanese traditional architecture, albeit not with these technical means. Glass shutters also open the upper levels to the exterior. With its operable openings and green wall, the Nicolas G. Hayek Center marks a departure from the more traditionally designed small towers that line Ginza. Its structural grid is underlined by the four main stacked blocks and the glazing of the movable shutters. Despite the narrow aspect of the building site, parking

for more than 30 cars is provided in two underground levels. The project manager for the Nicolas G. Hayek Center was Nils Kröger from Hayek Engineering, who was also the overall project manager for the Swatch and Omega buildings in Biel/Bienne. His deputy for the Tokyo project, Niels Knandel, also managed the Swatch Headquarters building construction between 2012 and 2019, underlining the continuity that has characterized the collaboration between Shigeru Ban and Hayek Engineering. Taro Okabe, who was the main on-site architect for the Bienne buildings, was also involved in the Tokyo project for Shigeru Ban Architects.

2006 **Centre Pompidou-Metz**
2010 Metz, France

The decision to create an extension to the Centre Pompidou in the eastern city of Metz was taken in January 2003 by then Minister of Culture Jean-Jacques Aillagon and the President of the Centre Pompidou, Bruno Racine. On May 27, 2003, the competition jury, which included the architect Richard Rogers, reduced the original 157 entries to six, including Foreign Office Architects (FOA), Herzog & de Meuron, and Dominique Perrault; Shigeru Ban teamed with Jean de Gastines from Paris and Gumuchdjian Architects (London). Ban's team won the competition

in November of the same year. The program for the facility included large public areas on the ground floor, above which Shigeru Ban suspended three 90 x 15-meter gallery "tubes." The most surprising aspect of the building is its undulating timber roof, inspired in part by a Chinese bamboo hat that Ban had purchased in Paris in 1998. "This story actually goes back to the time I was working with Frei Otto on the Japanese Pavilion in Hanover," says Shigeru Ban. "I saw his Institute for Lightweight Structures (Stuttgart, 1966–67). This is a cable structure, but it uses a lot of wood. The cables just form a net and beneath it he needed a surface, so he put a lot of timber behind. My thought was that a structure like this could exist just with the timber, without any cables behind. You need a surface, so why not combine its functions to create the structure as well? This realization brought me back to the bamboo hat. I of course admire the work of Frei Otto, but I wanted to do something different. We needed a surface, so why have cables as well? I always like to use material as little as possible. My first thought was to

have a big roof that would have extended over a garden in Metz."[1] After he won the competition for the Metz building, Shigeru Ban obtained permission to build his Paper Temporary Studio on the sixth-floor roof terrace of the Centre Pompidou in Paris in 2004. This structure permitted the architects to be in close contact with the Centre Pompidou at the same time as it gave visitors a chance to look in on the actual work process that went into the Metz building. This 115-square-meter temporary office, a paper-tube structure with some timber and steel, had a roof made of titanium dioxide PTFE membrane, regular PTFE (polytetrafluoroethylene) membrane, and PVC membrane.

1. Shigeru Ban in conversation with the author, Paris, July 23, 2008.

Haesley Nine Bridges Golf Clubhouse
Yeoju, South Korea

The Nine Bridges Country Club–Clubhouse is a 16,000-square-meter facility that was built to serve a golf course located two hours southeast of Seoul. Sitting on a base made of locally sourced random rubble masonry, the partial timber structure has a basement and three levels above grade. There is a main building, VIP lobby building, and a structure with private suites. The three-story atrium and the upper portion of the main building include timber columns and a glass curtain wall. The first floor of the atrium has 4.5-meter-wide glass shutters that open fully, in a gesture reminiscent of other buildings by Shigeru Ban, such as the Centre Pompidou-Metz (see p.38). The space is used for reception, a member's lounge, and a party area. The stone podium is used for locker rooms, bathrooms, and service areas. The 2,592-square-meter, double-curved roof was made with glulam timber that was manufactured in Switzerland. The unusual tree-like timber columns in the atrium reach the full height of three stories. The roof has a circular three-meter-diameter skylight above each column. The partial-timber structure was intended to conform to Korean regulations that do not allow timber buildings to exceed 6,000 square meters in size. As he did for the Centre Pompidou-Metz, Tamedia building, Seine Musicale, and the Swatch/Omega campus, Shigeru Ban called here on the Swiss wood engineer Hermann Blumer. As is frequently the case in his buildings, Ban mixes elements of local tradition, such as the stone base and wooden structure, with a very present modernity, highlighted by the glass curtain walls and the sense of open space in the atrium area. Especially as seen from a distance, the flat roof and full-height glazing also bring to mind the

Modernist simplicity of some works of Ludwig Mies van der Rohe, for example his Neue Nationalgalerie in Berlin (1968), although the roof designed by Mies is, of course, in steel and not in wood.

2011
2013

Tamedia
Zurich, Switzerland

This 10,120-square-meter headquarters building was designed for 480 employees of the largest media group in Switzerland. Now called TX Group, the firm owns daily and weekly newspapers, magazines, digital platforms, and has its own printing facilities. The so-called Werdareal site where the new headquarters building is located has been the home of the Group since 1902 when the Tages-Anzeiger newspaper was installed there. The main structural system designed by Shigeru Ban for the new TX Group offices relies on timber and seeks to meet the most demanding Swiss environmental standards. The 3,600 spruce trees used for the building come from neighboring forests.

The wood was milled using CNC technology in nearby Gossau. In Zurich, construction workers assembled the structure using no screws, nails, or steel connectors. Instead, bolts made with harder beech wood were used to stabilize the lattice-shaped wood structure. Fire protection was augmented in consultation with local services. The idea of openness and innovation sought both by the client and the architect resulted in the choice of glass façades, giving the structure "a unique appearance from the interior space as well as from the surrounding city." Set on a 1,000-square-meter site in central Zurich on the Sihl Canal, the seven-story structure has an added area in a two-floor extension on the roof of an earlier contiguous building that also belongs to the Group. Lounge areas and vertical links between the different office stories, which can be used as informal meeting and rest areas, are part of Ban's design. These spaces have a façade composed of retractable glass windows that allow transformation into open-air terraces. The height of the building and the mansard configuration of the roof were determined in part by local building regulations, although the architect used a glazed and louvered covering for the roof that allows ample light to penetrate the flexible spaces below. This somewhat unusual solution is very much in keeping with the building as a whole, which has the appearance of a more "normal" modern office building while using innovative structural systems and providing a real feeling of being in keeping with the times. Completed in 2013, the Tamedia building was Shigeru Ban's first completed work in Switzerland.

2014
2017   La Seine Musicale
Île Seguin, Boulogne-Billancourt, France

The Seine Musicale is located at the western tip of the Île Seguin, formerly the location of a large Renault automobile factory. The name "Seine," that of the river on which the island is located, is a play on words in French, pronounced the same way as *scène*, which is the word for "stage." The 280-meter-long site, which occupies about a third of the island, was originally intended for the François Pinault Foundation designed by Tadao Ando (2000), and the 36,500-square-meter Seine Musicale is inserted into an overall master plan for the island conceived by Jean Nouvel. Built like his other more recent French projects with the local architect Jean de Gastines, the

building has a prominent "sail," a curving form mounted on rails that turns according to the orientation of the sun and that is covered with 470 photovoltaic panels. The sail curves above a glazed hexagonal grid-shell wooden dome that covers the 1,150-square-meter classical music concert hall. The hall has birch plywood walls, solid oak floors, and a ceiling made from wood hexagons filled with paper tubes and suspended from an acoustic reflector to enhance the acoustics. As Shigeru Ban explains the glazing of the dome: "Its color changes from emerald green to bronze red according to the lighting and the angle of vision. It is inspired from the Japanese *tamamushi* beetle." The multipurpose 4,000-seat Grande Seine concert hall, intended for amplified music, can accommodate as many as 6,000 persons. It sits below a landscaped green roof. The complex includes a choir school, a rooftop garden, and a 1,475-square-meter sculpture garden at the tip of the Île Seguin. Built at a cost of 170 million euro by the Department of the Hauts-de-Seine, the complex is under the programmatic control of STS Evènements, a joint venture between the television station TF1 and Sodexo, a health-services company. Artists in residence include Laurence Equilbey and the Insula Orchestra, Gaël Darchen and La Maîtrise des Hauts-de-Seine, and Philippe Jaroussky and his Académie Musicale. The forms and the composition of the Seine Musicale are certainly unusual, but they are, as is almost always the case with Shigeru Ban, a response to specific programmatic and site considerations. Despite the architect's indication that ecological considerations are not paramount for him, the Seine Musicale is clearly an environmentally friendly building.

SWATCH HEADQUARTERS

Since the creation of the Swatch Group, Swatch itself had not had its own headquarters building, instead occupying spaces on the Omega campus in the bilingual town of Biel/Bienne until a 2010 competition was launched to design a home for the world-straddling brand. With developing demand for Omega watches coming from Asia and other parts of the world, it was also determined that a new factory for the brand was required. A third volume, intended as a brand museum and conference center, was added to the program of the invited architecture competition that Shigeru Ban won in the summer of 2011 and completed in October 2019.

The 25,016-square-meter Swatch Headquarters has four stories above ground level and a basement parking area for 170 cars and 182 bicycles. The front area of the building includes a 22-meter-high lobby, showrooms, and customer service. The central part of the Headquarters houses the offices of the administration, management, marketing, sales, and associated departments. The rear of the building, which provides space for storage and deliveries, opens toward Rue Jakob-Stämpfli. As seen from the exterior, this curving building has been described as "reptilian." But this is not a free-form in the recent sense of extravagant computer-generated oddities. Instead, it is a thoroughly rational solution to a complex series of problems. More interesting still, behind the curved roof and walls of the Swatch Headquarters, there is a carefully conceived grid design. The roof itself is a feat of timber engineering, at once complex and obvious in its logic.

A Curve and a Grid

The curved timber grid-shell roof of the office and warehouse building, which is 240 meters long, 35 meters wide, and as high as 27 meters, covers open concrete floors and also spans Rue Nicolas G. Hayek to become the roof of the conference hall that sits on top of the Cité du Temps building. With a 30-kilometer-per-hour speed limit for automobile traffic, the street also allows pedestrians to readily walk from the Swatch building to the Omega campus to the west. With its forms largely determined by three different local building height regulations and setback requirements for the site, the timber roof is arranged according to a 2.1 x 2.1-meter grid. Although Shigeru Ban has designed other rather freely curving roofs, such as the one of the Centre Pompidou-Metz (France, 2010; see p.38), his entire three-building project in Bienne for Swatch and Omega does not follow a predictable scheme of curvature. Instead, he resorts to more rectilinear and then completely orthogonal plans and elevations beginning in the second building, the Cité du Temps, and ending in the Omega Factory. Subverting the image of modern architecture that would have called for these buildings to be built in steel and concrete, Shigeru Ban makes use of engineered, load-bearing wood in all three structures.

Behind the curved roof and walls of the Swatch Headquarters, there is a carefully conceived grid design.

In the interview published in this volume (see p.21), Shigeru Ban underlines that Japan has an almost unequaled mastery of traditional woodworking, including for wooden buildings. Although the Swatch Headquarters uses very few metal connecting elements, it is less a reflection of the architect's Japanese origins than it is a testimony to the advanced wood engineering that has developed in Germany and Switzerland. Glulam columns and beams and cross-laminated timber slabs are the stuff of this building, rather than any hand-carved elements made of solid wood. Using parametric design and CNC milling, vast numbers of different wooden pieces were manufactured to exacting standards, creating a very different wooden building than might have been feasible just a few years earlier. These systems make possible a variation of no more than 19 millimeters over the 240-meter curved length of the structure; a standard that more conventional buildings would be hard put to equal.

The Swiss wood engineer Hermann Blumer and Shigeru Ban in conversation. On the left, Christoph Meier, a structural engineer who works with Blumer.

Bright, Unencumbered Space

The Swatch Headquarters is filled with light, starting with its high lobby, and glazing that rises up the façade/roof from a height of 5.5 meters to a maximum of 22 meters. Nine balconies, ranging in size from 10 to 20 square meters, further enhance the relation of users to the green surroundings. It is what another Japanese architect calls a "roof building," one whose defining feature is the roof. In this case, the roof and the walls are one, curving from the highest point of the structure down to the ground. Where the roof of a typical building allows in little natural light, here the arcing roof, which also constitutes the main façades, lets in light at every possible occasion, passing into opacity only to better control solar gain. With this building,

The area beneath the roof of the Swatch Headquarters can be rearranged freely to make space for meetings of various sizes or individual workspaces.

Shigeru Ban gives an insight into his relations with the work of such figures as Buckminster Fuller and Frei Otto. Like the celebrated geodesic domes designed by the former, with their arching lightness and material economy, like the spider-web forms of the 1972 Munich Olympic Stadium imagined by the latter, Ban's all-encompassing roof may be unexpected at first glance, but on closer examination makes eminent good sense. In his own oeuvre, Shigeru Ban references the Japanese Pavilion in Hanover (2000; see p.35) which gave a similar sense of unencumbered, indeed spectacular, interior space. Naturally, in Bienne, confronted with a permanent structure, the architect has to create a more solid shell, and he did this in close collaboration with the wood engineer Hermann Blumer. Inside, the vast column-free spaces of the building are exhilarating and, perhaps even more important for a large company, completely flexible and adaptable to future development.

Both Modest and Audacious

Where it would seem that computer-driven contemporary architecture has explored nearly every conceivable form, Shigeru Ban relies in a willful manner not on steel, but on wood, precisely because wood does impose certain limits. He calls on computer-assisted design, which has been developing rapidly for engineered wood, but this work is still more in contact with the rules of nature than would have been a steel design. From the town regulations that impose setbacks and varying height limits, to the requirements of the client, the architect imagines a solution. And this solution addresses not only practical elements, but also the spirit of Swatch, "playful and colorful" as he puts it. More than being satisfied with a conventional solution, Shigeru Ban goes further, combining the client's required three buildings into one for Swatch, and creating a roof that crosses over a street linking the Swatch Headquarters to the Cité du Temps, and also echoing and literally connecting to the stricter ethos of Omega. Ban's solution is architectural, but it is also philosophical and at the same time it breaks new ground, bringing nature, in the form of wood, into the equation. Unlike a steel design, wood exudes a certain warmth, which is augmented by the near omnipresence of filtered natural light, and views to the exterior. Working with the landscape architecture firm that also created a neighboring park, Ban succeeds in integrating his surprising Swatch Headquarters into the evolution and modernization of the urban environment of Bienne, which is, in other respects, a fairly staid and conventional town. In the place of a rambling garden center, the city has proudly embraced the innovative new headquarters of one of the most successful watchmakers in the world. The formula here achieves an equilibrium between modesty, with a natural side, and audacity that curves and leaps across a street.

> **Ban's solution breaks new ground, bringing nature, in the form of wood, into the equation.**

It might be felt that Shigeru Ban's "reptilian" Swatch Headquarters does not achieve the kind of harmony often sought in contemporary architecture. It is unexpected, even edging toward a kind of aggressivity as it opens into a high lobby and then flows across the street to cap the neighboring building, which is otherwise largely rectilinear. But the implacable logic of each gesture wins out in the end, making each element finally comprehensible, even if visitors are sometimes taken aback at the outset. Like the Centre Pompidou-Metz, the Swatch Headquarters does not bring to mind any immediate comparison to other buildings, unless one ventures into the work of Frei Otto and a few others. Shigeru Ban is not an engineer, but he calls on some of the best engineers in the world to bring his ideas to fruition. This engineering intelligence is also a signature of his work—it may look different, but it works, and in the case of Swatch it provides sensational office space, vast and inviting while still within the realm of the human scale.

ETFE, CLT, and FPO

Taro Okabe, the lead architect working on the overall Swatch/Omega project for Shigeru Ban, explains that the major focus of the design of the

Swatch Headquarters was indeed on its timber roof. He says: "Originally the idea was to build an entirely transparent roof, 100% covered with ETFE (ethylene tetrafluoroethylene) cushions with air inside of them. In fact, the roof cannot be 100% transparent because of excessive solar gain. In the final solution there are opaque panels, glass panels, and ETFE panels, allocated according to needs." No less than 2,800 unique panels were needed to cover the 11,000-square-meter surface of the flowing roof. For the opaque panels, more concentrated at the top of the roof, Swiss cross forms were introduced to brace the structure and to contain acoustic absorbers to maintain the required reverberation time in the office space, as well as to absorb traffic noise from Rue Nicolas G. Hayek. Transparent panels on the sides of the building offer views of the neighboring park. As Taro Okabe details the complexity of the design process: "The roof panels require building services—the ETFE panels need continuous compressed air, the glass panels have shading devices—so you need electricity and automation.

The Swatch Headquarters is a dynamically sustainable structure.

The glass elements also need compressed air because they are closed cavity façade panels and they need to be pressurized so that no dust comes inside. The solid panels are made with CLT (cross-laminated timber) slabs, steel plate, and an FPO (flexible polyolefin) waterproofing membrane. Inside, these are equipped with chilled ceiling panels." As Okabe suggests, although there are three primary cladding types, there are actually nine different sorts of panel—including the ones including operable shades, photovoltaics, or other solutions. Although Shigeru Ban states that ecological concerns are not his primary motivation for using wood, the Swatch Headquarters is a dynamically sustainable structure. Aside from the renewable aspect of the wood employed, the heating and cooling of the building uses a groundwater pumping system. A total of 1,770 square meters of photovoltaic panels further reduces energy consumption.

The complexity of the service conduits and other elements in the original façade design generated a thickness of 1.4 meters as opposed to the 900 millimeters imagined in the competition entry. Since the floor area inside is a function of the continuous roof and façade, and the setbacks did not allow the structure itself to expand, this calculation meant that the building would lose 400 square meters of floor area as opposed to the original scheme. Okabe continues: "As this was not acceptable, we had to change the façade design, which took us one year. We changed the ways in which we combined the different services, for example running the air pipes inside of the structure instead of having a separate layer."

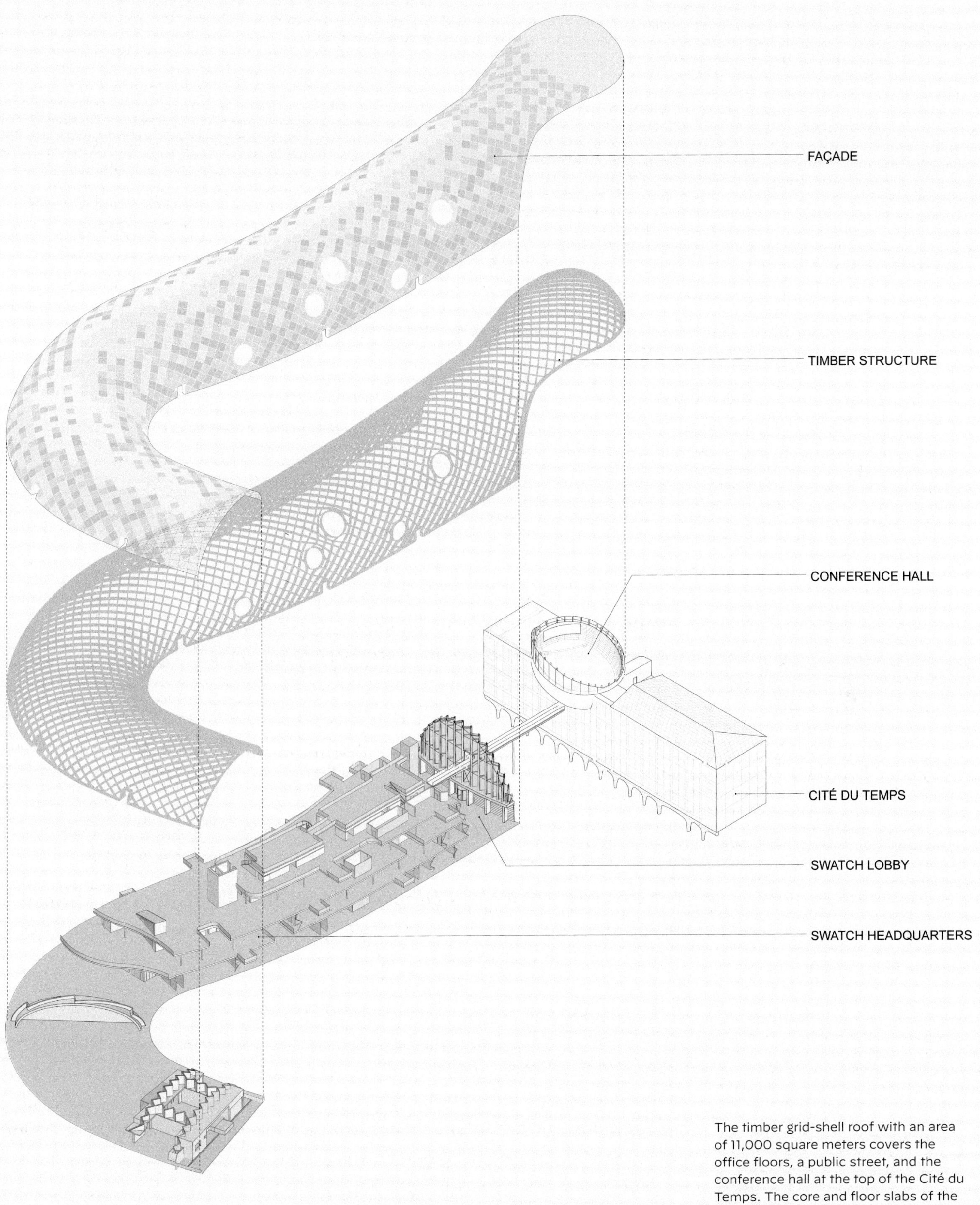

The timber grid-shell roof with an area of 11,000 square meters covers the office floors, a public street, and the conference hall at the top of the Cité du Temps. The core and floor slabs of the Swatch Headquarters are in concrete.

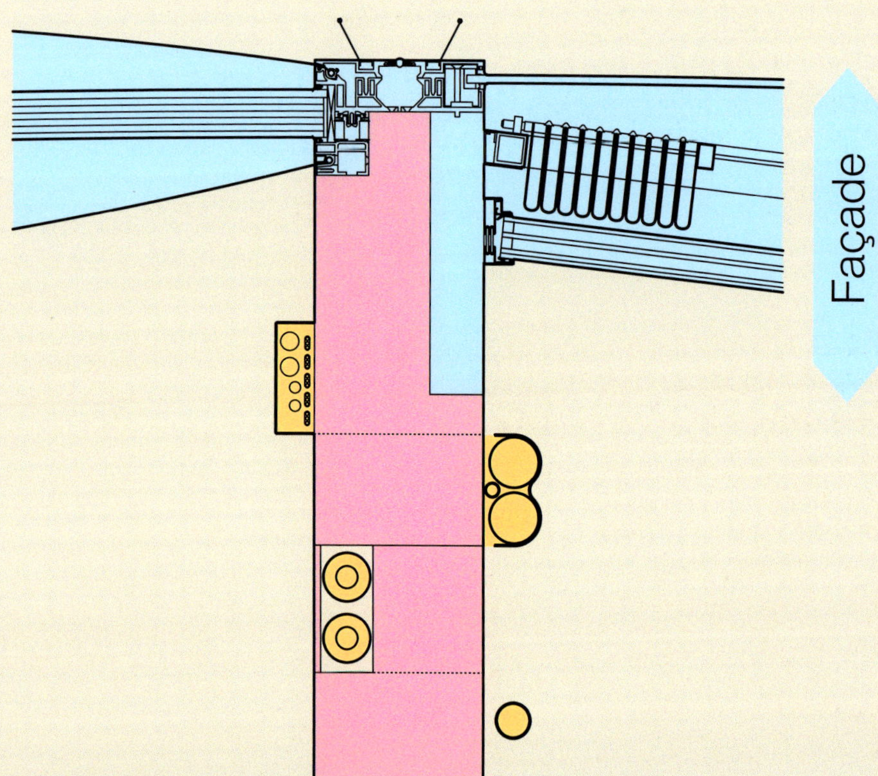

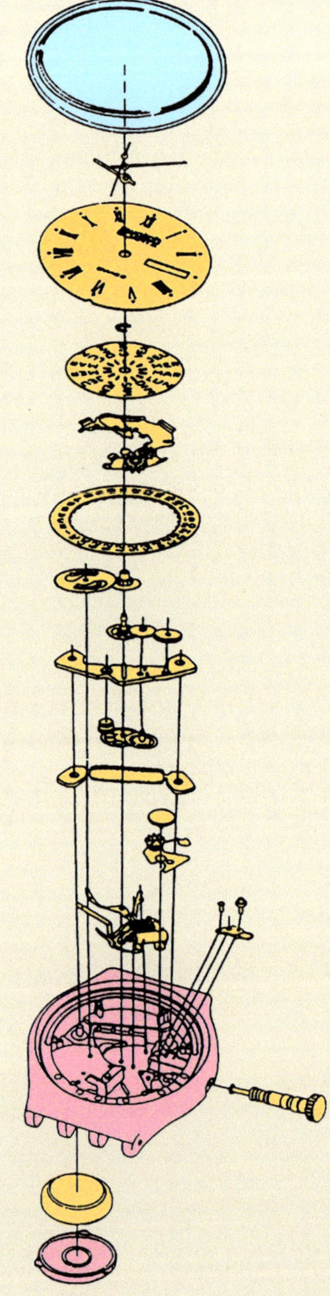

The roof structure of the Swatch Headquarters was conceived like a Swatch. The timber grid is precisely milled out to receive building service installations as well as façade elements. Both take advantage of the material, which allows precision machining or molding in the case of watches.

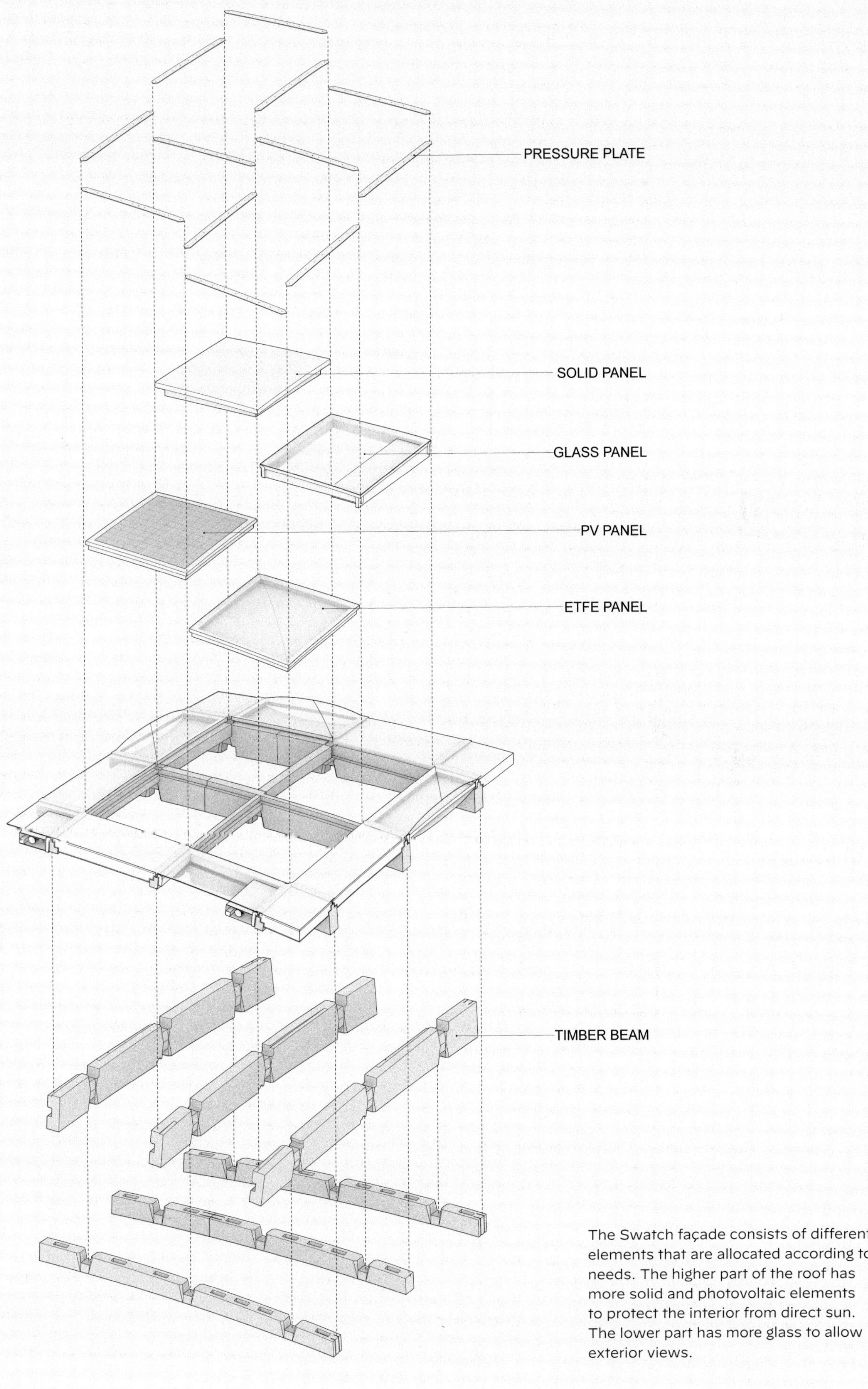

The Swatch façade consists of different elements that are allocated according to needs. The higher part of the roof has more solid and photovoltaic elements to protect the interior from direct sun. The lower part has more glass to allow exterior views.

Build It Like a Swatch

As the solution for the roof design imagined by Shigeru Ban and his teams evolved, it became apparent that it had striking similarities with the manufacturing innovations that made Swatch a success. "What is special for Swatch," says Taro Okabe, "is not so much that the watches are colorful but that they are assembled directly in the case. The plastic case is precisely manufactured to have all the holes and grooves in the right places, and this system permits the use of many fewer parts. This was only

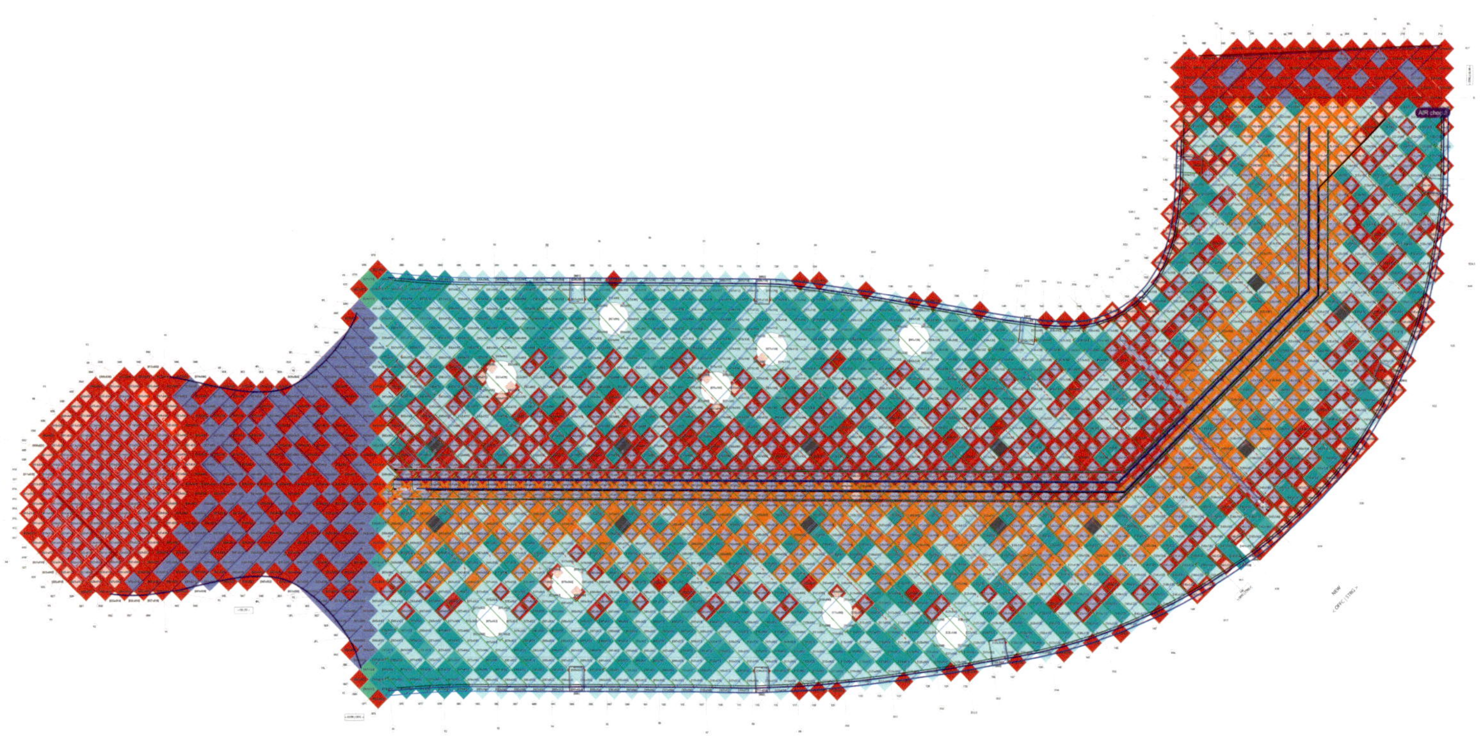

A flattened view that includes information related to the roof buildup: façade panel layout, building service connections to each panel, beam type, etc. All the specialists involved provided their input into this plan, and conflicts were highlighted automatically so that there would be no surprises on site. This drawing is linked to the parametric design that generated the individual wood elements.

possible with a plastic case because a metal one cannot be engraved with as much precision. A Swatch is assembled from 51 parts and that is why this project is called "SO51." The same ideas apply to our building. Wood allows for very high precision which lets us make grooves and holes and have each individual part manufactured in exactly the way we want. Even though we have 6,000 smaller parts for the façade, everything comes nicely together without great effort on site. We took advantage of wood just as Swatch took advantage of plastic as a new material for a watch. We did this using a parametric design system. A specialist writes a program and we give the forms of our building. The engineer calculates the height of the beam; the building service engineers indicate how the pipes should run;

and the program automatically generates the engineering drawings for each part. Without having people actually draw each little part, it is the computer program that generates the drawings." Of 62,792 prefabricated parts required for the roof, only 72 (0.11%) had errors as opposed to about 15% in more traditional building.

Bare Bones

As construction photos of the Swatch Headquarters reveal, the rather complex form of the curving grid-shell roof is actually what generates the exterior appearance of the building. If this appearance is not the kind of smooth, unified surface that much contemporary architecture supposes, it is precisely because Shigeru Ban eschews the conventional definitions of cladding, or rather says that he does not want to use cladding. Ban finds cladding as such to be artificial, the sort of thing one might put over an unattractive steel frame to make it look smooth and unified. Here, the variegated roof willfully reveals the different elements that make up the actual roof—ETFE cushions, solid panels for bracing and to house photovoltaics, and transparent glass, all serving actual functions that are not purely intended to make an impression as seen from the outside. This difference is important and is another factor that makes the work of Shigeru Ban look different from much other contemporary architecture. Elsewhere in the Swatch/Omega campus he shows, as he did for Tamedia (see p.41) in Zurich, that his wood designs can also result in more "normal" modern configurations, where rigorous wooden grids are covered in glass.

For the Swatch/Omega campus in general and the Swatch Headquarters in particular, Shigeru Ban had the advantage of being able to call on very high-quality Swiss materials and subcontractors. The wood is 100% Swiss and was manufactured in Switzerland by Blumer-Lehmann. A Zurich firm called Design to Production, specialized in 3-D, created the program used to generate the engineering drawings for the required parts but also mapped the different cladding elements, coordinating them with the appropriate timber components and building services as well as the related supply chains. A major change in the planning concept was thus required in order to achieve a drastic reduction of the roof thickness without compromising the performance of the façade. As the Swatch Group puts it: "The unusual design breaks with the conventions of classic office building architecture and blends harmoniously into the urban environment. The building's forms awaken the imagination—like a work of art, the interpretation lies in the eye of the beholder."

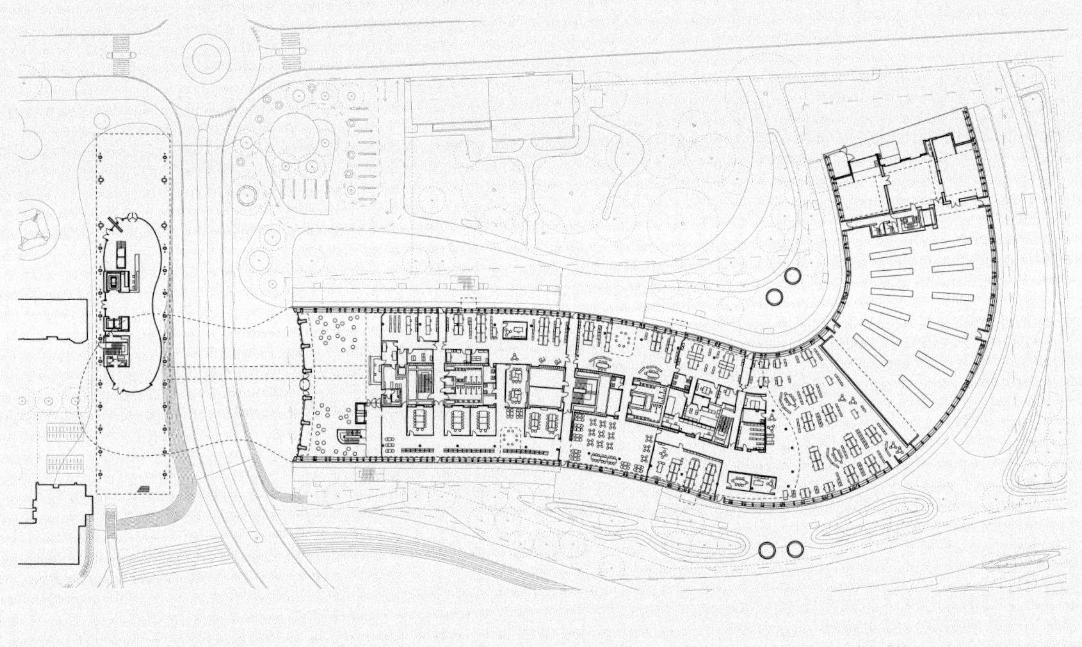

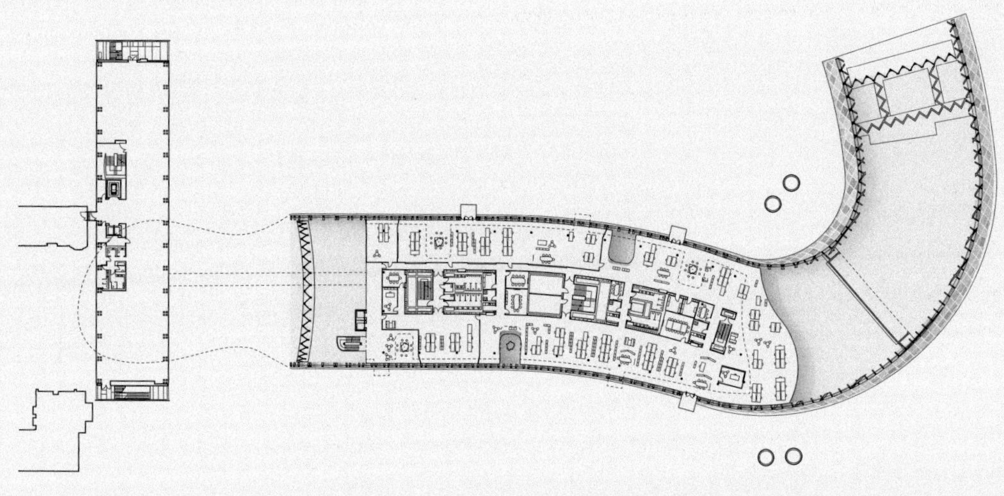

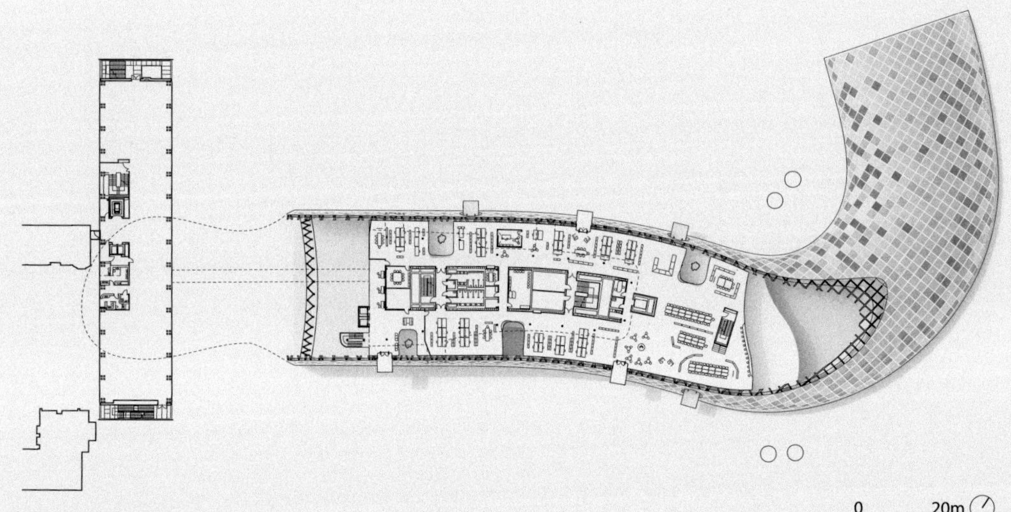

0   20m

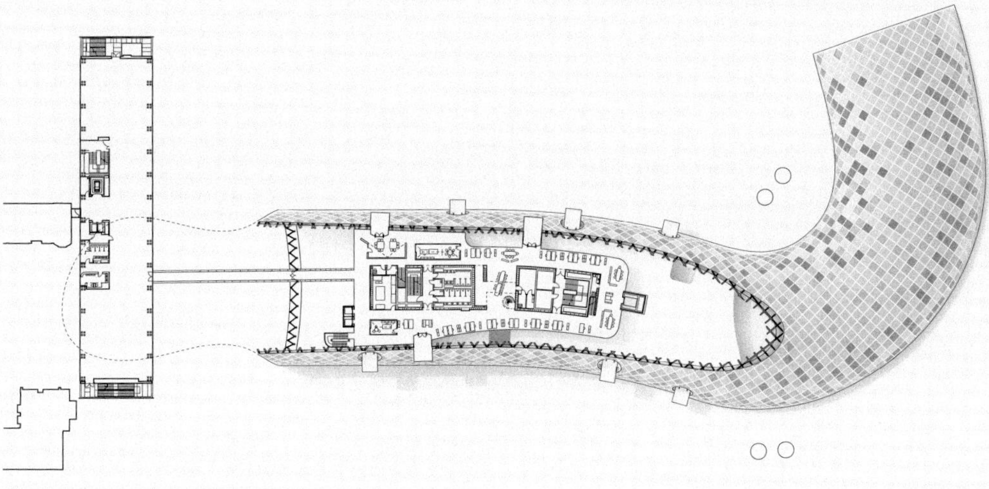

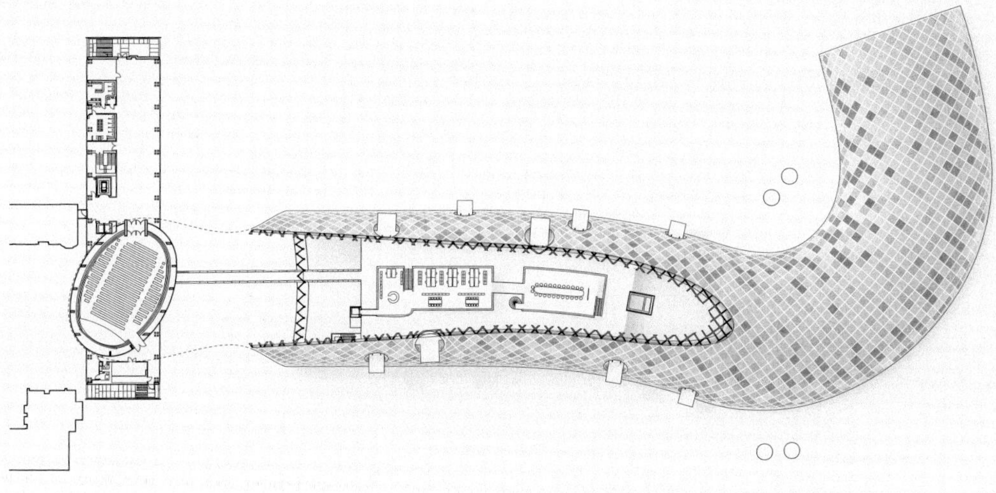

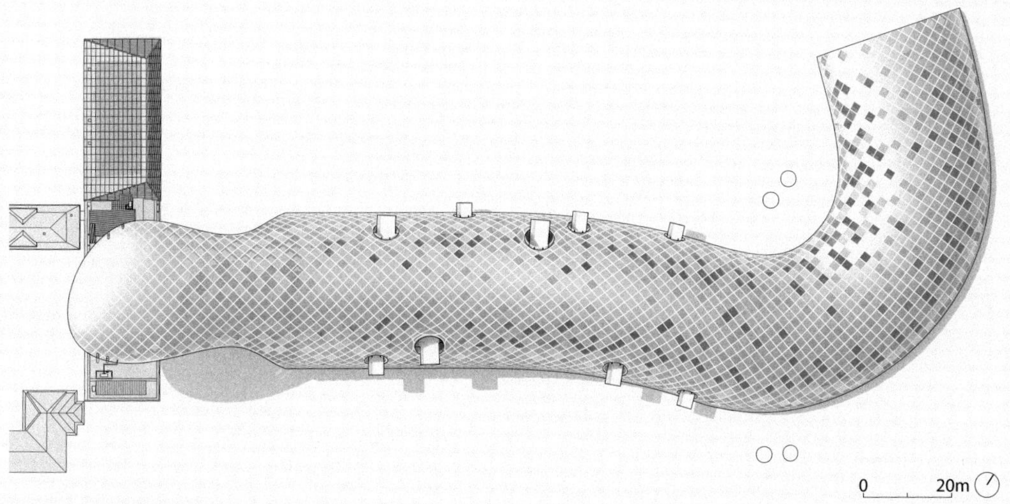

A site plan of the ground floor of the Swatch Headquarters and the Cité du Temps. The other drawings show each successive level of the two buildings and their link, which is formed by the footbridge and rooftop conference center.

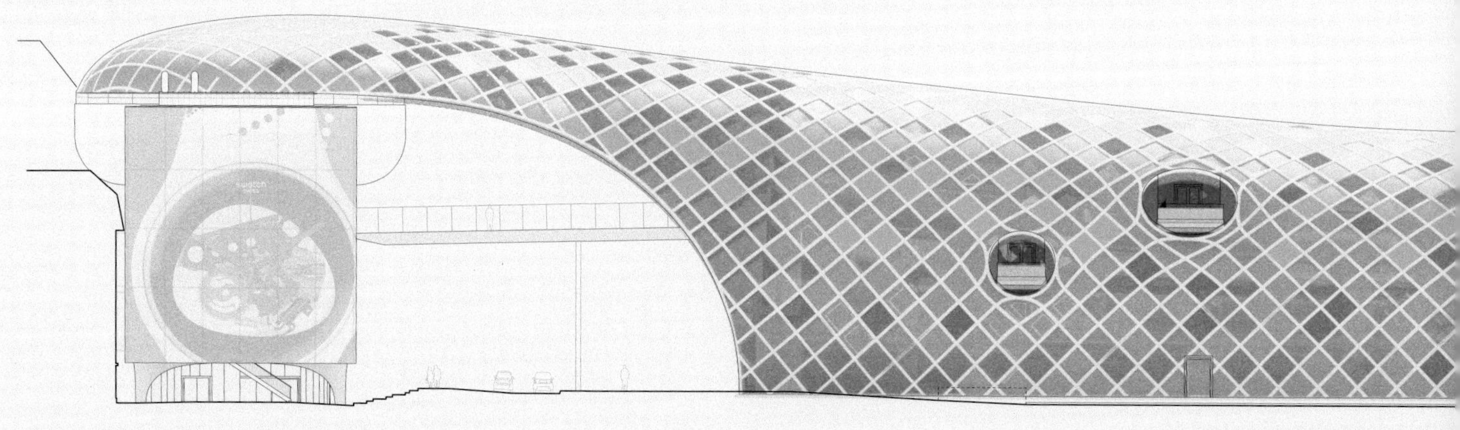

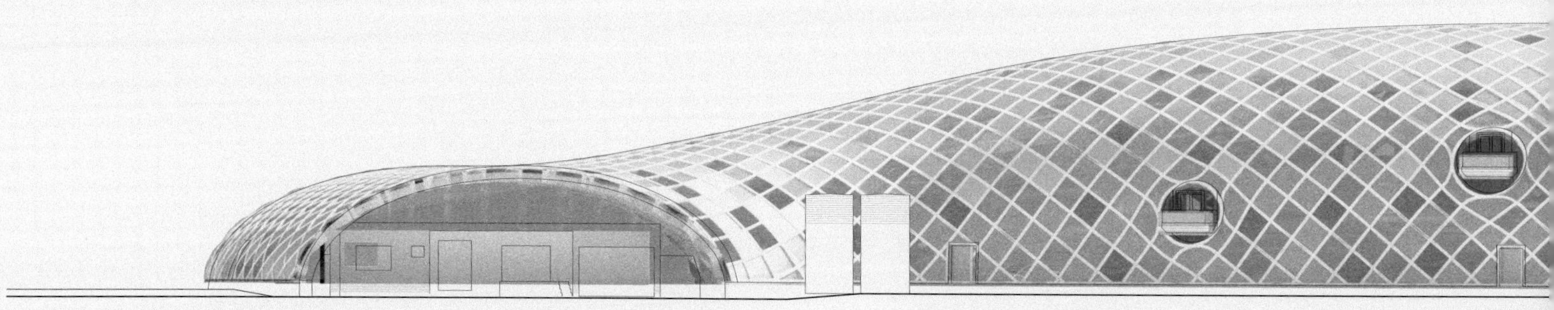

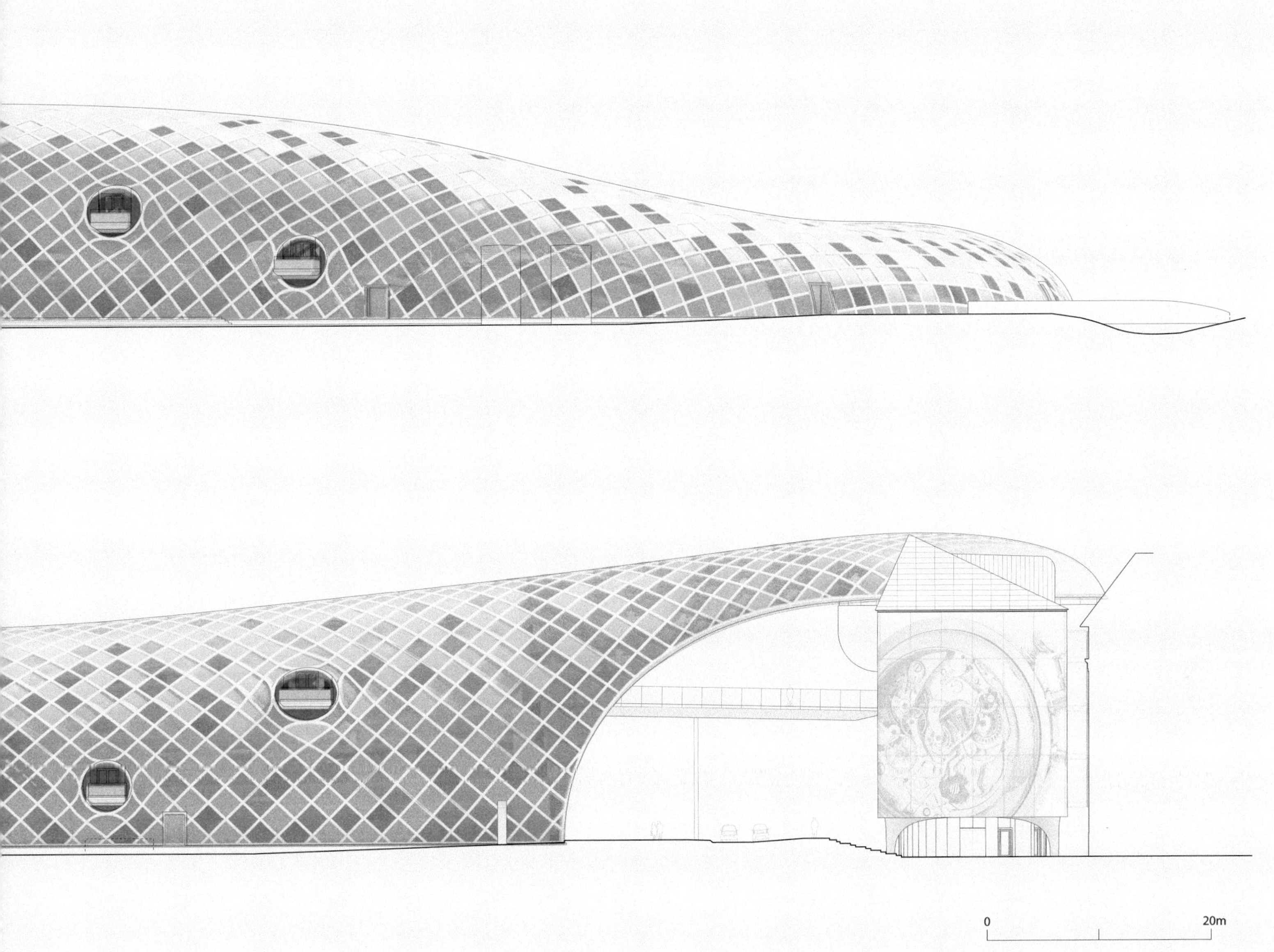

Long elevation
drawings of
the Swatch
Headquarters and
the connected
Cité du Temps
show cladding
patterns and the
balconies that
mark the curved
shell.

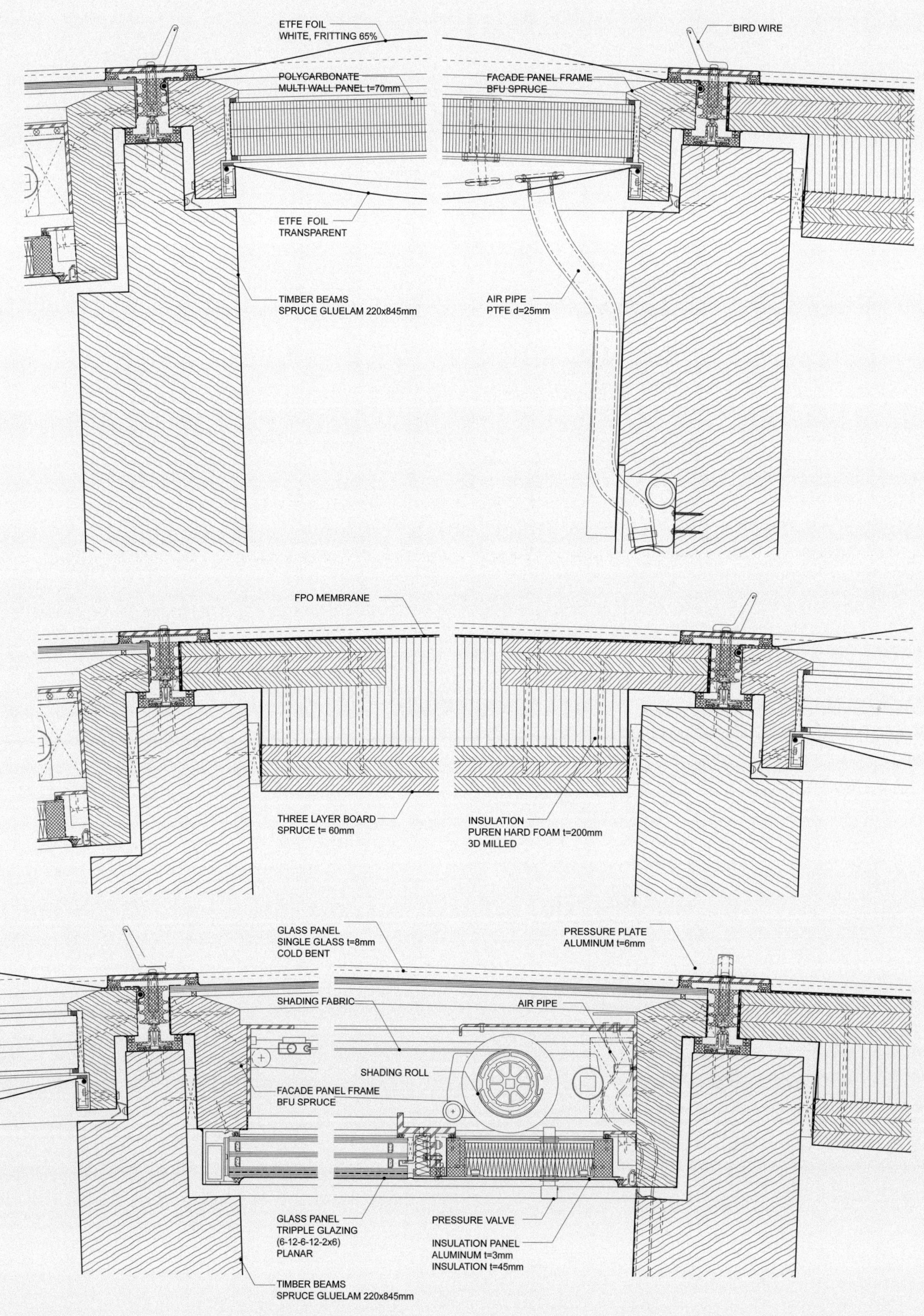

Details of three façade element types. Top: EFTE; middle:solid; bottom: transparent element.

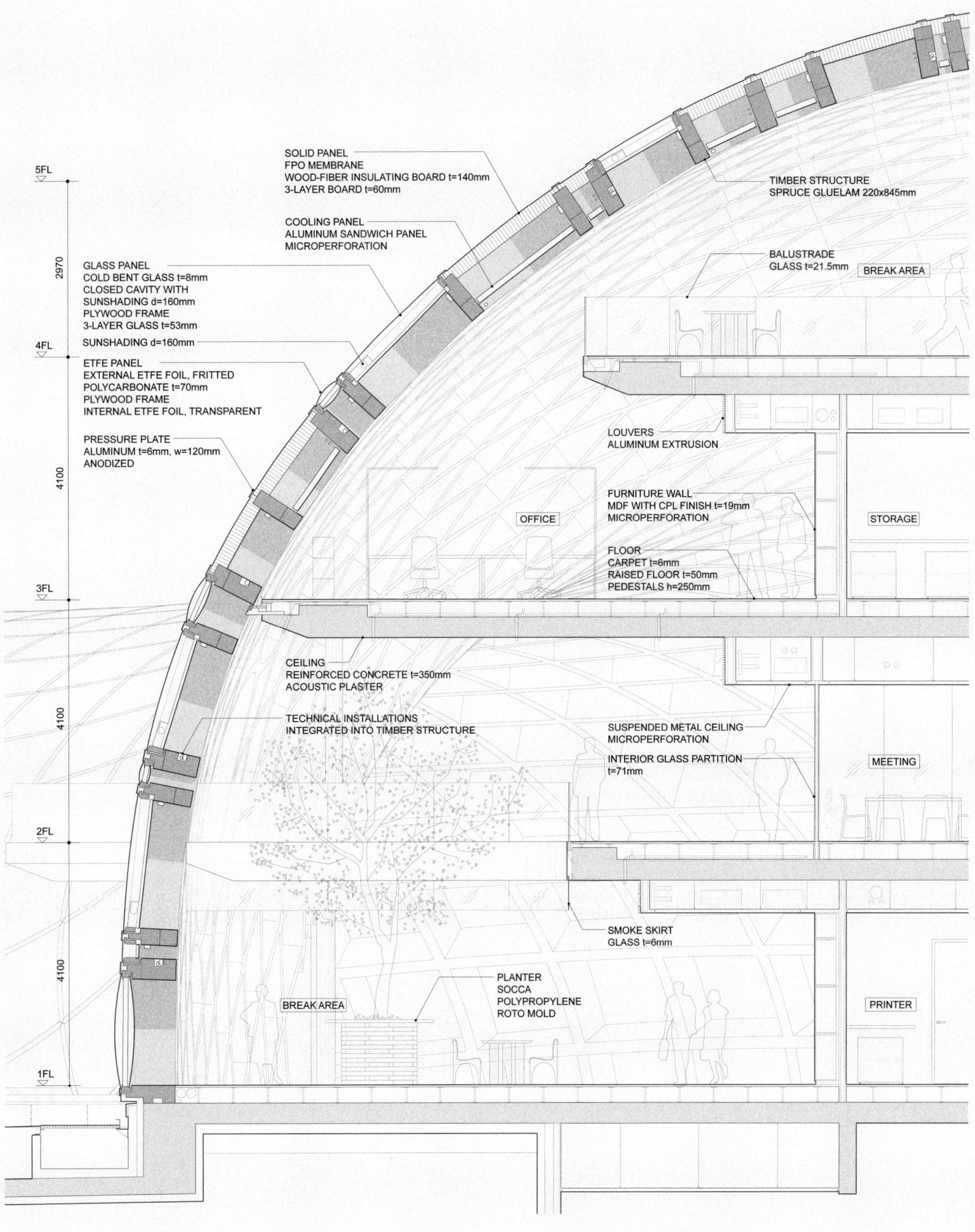

A detailed section drawing of the curved shell of the Swatch building showing the façade elements in place as well as the interior design.

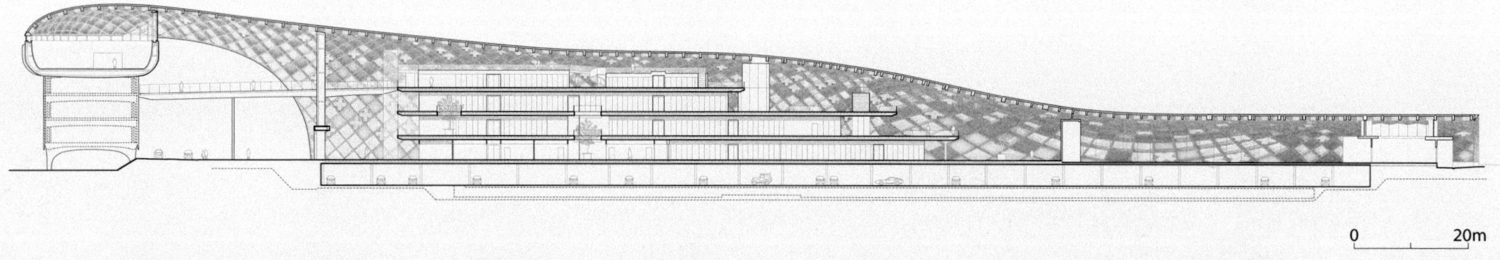

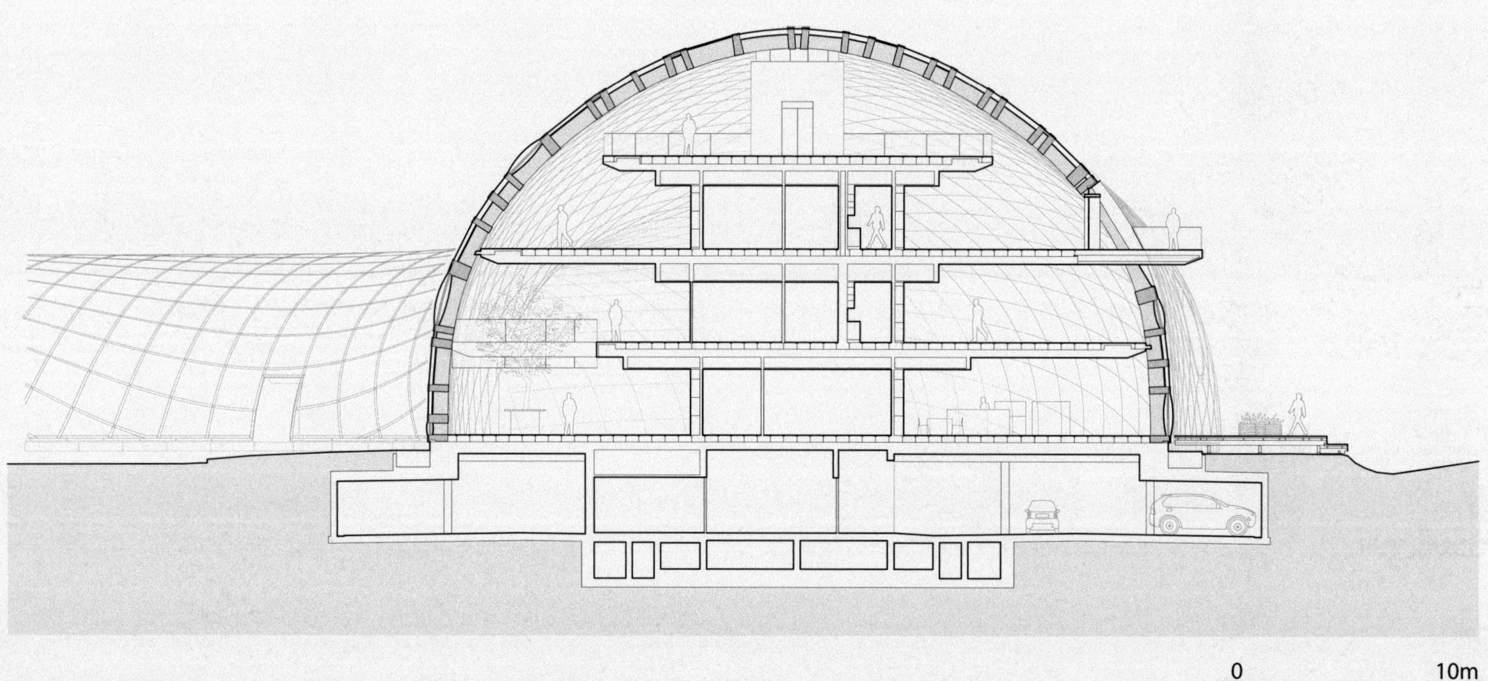

A long section of
the building (top)
and above, a cross
section.

The timber
elements being
assembled layer
by layer. The
longitudinal linear
beams clad in
white were used
as temporary
guides for the
assembly.

A drone view taken during construction. A two-story mock-up of part of the façade is visible near the roundabout. Even as the timber assembly advanced, the installation of the façade panels had begun at the front of the building.

Top: the second layer of roof elements is put in place.

Left: the third layer being installed. The small blocks seen on the underside of the beams are hardwood connectors that click into the first layer.

Right page: a specially designed "fork" was used to control the orientation of the hoisted timber elements.

Left page:
channels to
accommodate
building services
are visible on
the sides of the
beams being
installed in this
image.

Above: the glulam
beams near the
balcony openings
are doubly curved,
whereas the
majority of beams
in the structure
have a single
curvature.

Above: the precisely cut timber beams allowed for rapid and smooth assembly on site.

Right page: a glass element of the façade being installed. The triple glazing has a flat interior side with an external layer that is cold-bent to follow the organic shape of the shell.

Following double page: the layout of darker-colored photovoltaic elements was determined according to solar radiation analysis. The park along the river was designed by the same landscape architect involved in the Swatch and Omega sites.

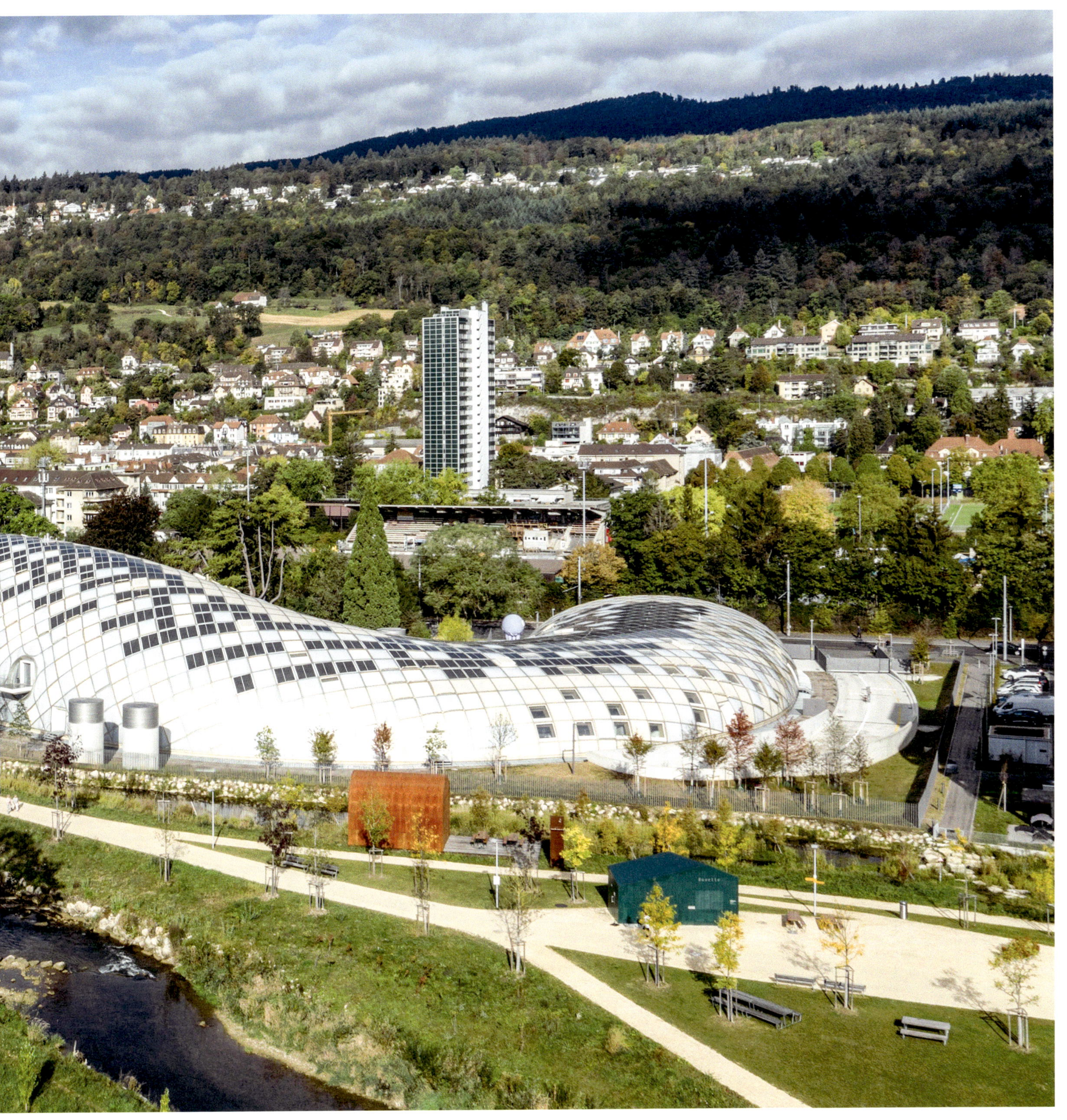

An elevated view from the east looking toward the Jura foothills, home to much of the Swiss watchmaking industry. The rounded building in the foreground is the Swatch Headquarters.

The pavement of
Rue Nicolas G.
Hayek becomes
lighter as it
passes between
the Swatch and
Omega sites. The
overall pavement
scheme of the
public areas
on the site is
the same to
emphasize the
continuity of the
campus.

Right page: the
entire façade
glows in the dark.
Some EFTE
elements are
operable, allowing
for the possibility
of natural
ventilation.

Left page:
view from the
connecting bridge.
The form of the
front façade was
determined by the
timber grid and
by an analysis of
potential wind
loads.

Above: the façade
of the building at
the main entrance
is equipped with
full-size operable
glass shutters
in a gesture
reminiscent of
buildings such
as the Centre
Pompidou-Metz.

The Swiss crosses
in the timber grid
act as acoustic
absorbers to
diminish traffic
noise. For special
occasions, the
street can be
closed and used
as an event space.

Left page: the EFTE panels on the underside of the roof as it crosses over the street are a simple two-layer cushion without a polycarbonate panel inside.

Above: the glass shutters at the entrance can be fully opened to create an open space from the Swatch lobby all the way to the Cité du Temps.

Left page: the ceiling height of the lobby is approximately 22 meters, here spanning the full 32-meter width of the building without any intermediate support.

Above: visible within the lobby, the timber footbridge that crosses over to the Cité du Temps. The dramatically curved timber elements give a dynamic aspect to the space, which has ample natural light.

Following double page: the lobby of the building with the overhead footbridge again visible. The space is generous and filled with light. The visible presence of wood warms a truly contemporary volume.

Top: all workstations are located within six meters of the façades to allow for sufficient natural light.

Left: in this fourth-floor view, the tops of the cores do not reach the timber roof but, instead, form islands with meeting rooms and offices.

Right page: trees planted in plastic elements designed by Shigeru Ban are located in floor openings to take advantage of the ceiling height.

The generous floor openings allow for visual connections between the different levels. The core wall furniture is color coded for the different floors as well as special functions, such as recycling, mailboxes, and fire hoses.

Above: the galleries facing the lobby space are main access paths to the offices and also function as waiting and gathering spaces.

Left: the entire core wall was covered with color-coded storage volumes.

Right page: longitudinal visibility was an important consideration in the design. This was achieved while, of course, respecting security and fire restrictions.

In this view from
the ground floor
at the end of
the office space
all the levels
of the building
are visually
connected.

LIMELIGHT

Left page: a
meeting room
on the fifth
level. A linear air
curtain along the
perimeter of this
space prevents
warm air from
rising into the
area.

Above: the forms
of the glass walls
create a variety of
sun patterns in the
lobby, enlivening
the space
and making it
constantly change
in appearance.

CITÉ DU TEMPS

The Cité du Temps is a long, narrow building (80 meters long and 17 meters wide) that is located across the street from the Swatch Headquarters in Biel/Bienne. It has a gross floor area of 7,061 square meters, including a basement, partial ground floor, and five upper levels which are in good part a glazed, timber, post-and-beam structure. Steel is very much a "supporting actor" in this building. It is used for external staircases at either end of the building and also for diagonal braces needed above the first floor to offset the irregular spacing of the concrete arches at ground level near Rue Jakob-Stämpfli and the load of the conference hall on the top floor.

While the client had suggested placing this building directly along Rue Jakob-Stämpfli, Shigeru Ban preferred to situate it along Rue Nicolas G. Hayek, lifting it off the ground on concrete arches and thus offering pedestrian access to the newly named Omega Plaza, which is set precisely where the original program imagined the footprint of the new building. The bridge over the street and the 30-kilometer-per-hour speed limit on that street actively encourage pedestrians, whether from the general public or the firms involved, to cross over and through the campus much more actively than had been possible in the past. The bridge is reserved to persons working for the Group. The transparent reception space of the Cité du Temps, with its ample curved glazing, is also inviting and open.

Museums and a Conference Hall

The Cité du Temps is the only publicly accessible structure on the Swatch/Omega campus and includes the Omega Museum on the first floor, Planet Swatch on the second floor, a flexible exhibition area on the third floor, and a conference hall on the top floor that accommodates 400 persons (in concert seating). The museum floors have column-free spaces that measure 15 meters in width by 70 meters in length. The load-bearing structure is visible in the groups of four 280-millimeter-square timber columns spaced five meters apart between the first and fourth floors. These columns allow for stable connections with 320-millimeter-wide wood girders and beams arriving from two different directions. Tasked with creating buildings for Swatch and Omega that were specific to the brands, Shigeru Ban made the Cité du Temps a link between the two. The timber grid-shell roof of the Swatch Headquarters crosses over Rue Nicolas G. Hayek, "landing" on the roof of the Cité du Temps where it covers and forms the oval conference hall volume that is inserted into the top floor. The timber pedestrian bridge also crosses over the street beneath the arching roof.

The transparent reception space of the Cité du Temps, with its ample curved glazing, is also inviting and open.

The timber columns that connect the conference hall bowl and the Swatch Headquarters grid-shell roof were designed in order to allow for a displacement of up to 80 millimeters. Aside from the area concerned by the grid shell of the conference hall, the roof of the Cité du Temps has a pitched roof that echoes older buildings on the Omega campus. The mechanical plant is situated beneath this pitched roof, whose exterior is used for photovoltaic panels.

The conference hall has an exterior cladding made with 1.5 million pieces of 2-centimeter-square Italian glass mosaic tiles. These tiles are pearl white on the side of the Omega campus and more colorful opposite the Swatch Headquarters, another nod to the different characters of the brands. Mosaic also appears beneath the conference hall on part of the third-floor ceiling and a fourth-floor wall, establishing a visual and material continuity between the exterior and interior of the volume. The interior walls of the conference hall are finished with solid white ash ribs with ventilation, air exhaust, and acoustic absorption provided for in between the ribs. The architect also designed the stage, speaker's podium, and four speaker tables also using white ash.

Wood Becomes Modern

Although the idea of a timber structure might bring to mind a relatively closed design, in the image of old wood buildings, and perhaps be contrary to the kind of modern transparency of curtain-wall structures, the Cité du Temps is very much the work of a new generation. Aside from the grafted, curving volume of the conference hall, the rest of the Cité du Temps is rectilinear or even Modernist in plan and section. It is bright and open and very much the product of a rigorous grid design and does have glass walls. Emphasizing its modern nature, a decision was taken to place all closed spaces—such as elevators, bathrooms, and machine rooms—on the south side of the building, allowing an open and transparent view of interior spaces through the glass façades from the street side and Omega Plaza. Partial external blinds and glazing with solar coating allow the timber structure to remain visible and even transparent with night lighting.

Detail view of the two-centimeter-square Italian glass mosaic tiles that cover the conference center. The color of this cladding shifts from east (Swatch) to west (Omega).

Precision in Every Detail

With the Cité du Temps, Shigeru Ban again largely avoids cladding in any opaque sense. With the exception of the mosaic covering of the bowl of the conference hall, the Cité du Temps is entirely glazed and its wooden elements are proudly exhibited, not only making it fully clear that this is a timber building, but also showing most precisely how it was put together. Ban clearly places an emphasis on the structural design that underlies his work, never wishing to disguise it. For him, the architect does not create a seductive object so much as take on a complex problem and solve it using the simplest and purest means possible. Here, he selects one of the oldest building materials—wood—and uses it in new ways. In many respects, engineered and CNC milled wood is a new construction material. It can be shaped in almost any way, within certain limits. It is precisely the lack of limits implied by a steel structure that Ban rejects—he wants limits and then he tries to expand on those limits using technology and architectural imagination. The structure is the message in some sense, and this structure serves the program, and even improves on what the client might have imagined.

Wooden columns and girders create an open space that spans 15 meters. The girders were made by laminating pre-bent members and cutting the upper ends straight in order to avoid deflection.

The basic structural material is locally sourced timber. The main structural elements—glulam (glue-laminated timber) and CLT (cross-laminated timber) panels—are made with spruce, with some parts in beech, a hard wood that offers greater structural strength. The total quantity of timber used in the building was 1,618 cubic meters. Even the elevator shaft is made of spruce CLT panels. On the western side of the Cité du Temps, CLT slabs are cantilevered from museum floors to create bridges connecting with the existing Omega D Building, originally a watch factory built by the architects Saager & Frey in 1917. This system avoids applying added loads to the historic building and allows free upper-level movement from the Swatch Headquarters into the Omega complex.

The basic structural material is locally sourced timber.

The grinding and cutting of the timber elements was executed with a high degree of accuracy by CNC machines providing in advance for the positioning of ducts and pipes and the junctions that support the glass curtain wall. The precise location and dimension of the cutouts that penetrate girders were determined by engineers from the start of the initial design stage, allowing the size and strength of girders to be determined with precision. The timber structure is certified to resist fire for at least 60 minutes. This result was achieved in collaboration with the engineers and involves oversizing the timber and adding joint details that prevent the spread of fire. Fire-rated glass partitions around the stairways are further protected by timber-veneer-clad fire board. Echoing the gentle natural aspect of the timber building, a hydronic (liquid) radiant heating and cooling system is used in all the spaces except the ground-floor reception.

A Movable Feat

One unexpected aspect of the construction was the creation and use by the firm Blumer-Lehmann of five-meter-wide wooden scaffolding, corresponding to the column spacing in the building. As each post-and-beam span was completed, the scaffolding was moved by a crane to the next assembly point. This system allowed the scaffolding itself to serve as a guide for the assembly at the same time as it supported columns and girders during assembly. Another unusual aspect of the construction was that the curtain walls were installed even before the timber construction was completed in order to protect the timber from the weather and to speed the overall process.

Continuity Throughout

The concrete arches at the base of the Cité du Temps of course allow pedestrians to pass beneath the building. These arches and the thin columns that support the building were made with laminated timber formwork prepared by a CNC machine. A system made with a steel frame and rail permitted the formwork to be used repeatedly. Yellow pigment and a "slight grain appearance" was added to the concrete, making its relation to the timber structure above more harmonious. The idea of design continuity in fact permeates the building. The reception area that occupies part of the ground floor echos this openness with generous curved glazing. Inside, the emphasis in the reception area is on design continuity. Tabletops are covered in the same marble used in the staircase and entrance hall wall, with vertical elements finished in Corian.

From One Cité to Another

In a typically indirect way, the Cité du Temps brings to mind the Cité Radieuse by Le Corbusier (Unité d'Habitation, Marseille, France, 1952), which has rounded concrete *pilotis* at ground level and sculptural elements on the roof. Although it is larger than the Cité du Temps (137 meters long, 24 meters wide and 56 meters high), the Cité Radieuse also has a narrow, rectangular plan. It can be noted in passing that Le Corbusier's Villa Savoye (Poissy, France, 1931) also lifts a rectilinear volume off the ground on reinforced-concrete *pilotis* and has a roof terrace marked by curvilinear walls. The name Cité du Temps was apparently selected by the client, so Shigeru Ban cannot be suspected of directly referencing Le Corbusier with this name, but there are clearly some intriguing parallels between the buildings, and one very major difference. That difference is, of course, Ban's use of timber for almost the entire structure, together with the very sophisticated computer-driven milling techniques required to achieve such precision. However, the curving elements on the roof of the Cité Radieuse can, indeed, bring to mind the surprising oval conference hall with its vaulting grid-shell roof on the Cité du Temps. The flat roof of the Cité Radieuse has sculptural ventilation stacks, a running track, a pool for children, and an art school recently transformed into an exhibition center called the MaM. Aside from the ventilation stacks, these elements do not respond to a structural or functional imperative, whereas the conference hall designed by Shigeru Ban was a program requirement and forms a physical connection between the "playfulness" of Swatch and the "rigor" of Omega, linking the two brand campuses. The Cité du Temps is thus a kind of hybrid, a Modernist body with a playful head. This makes perfectly good sense within the Swatch/Omega campus, the client's original request to differentiate the brands, and Shigeru Ban's desire to create links and open passageways. Shigeru Ban, like Le Corbusier, seeks to question and redefine modern architecture, and this is precisely what he has done with the Cité du Temps.

Top: the support
system with a
moveable steel
frame and rails
enabled the
repetitive use of
formwork.

Right: formwork
and rebars for
the ground-
floor concrete
arches. Three-
dimensional
curved formwork
was made by
shaving laminated
timber.

Challenges of Design and Construction

Yoshie Narimatsu, a Senior Associate at Shigeru Ban Architects who was responsible for the Cité du Temps, concludes: "This building is important because it connects two different campuses and two different brands and also includes the 17 brands of the Swatch Group, because the Cité du Temps is owned neither by Swatch nor by Omega but by the Swatch Group. From our point of view, the building had to create a visual, physical, and philosophical connection between the brands." Asked to outline the challenges of the designs and some of the most significant innovations in the project, Narimatsu continues: "The building has a basic rectangular form which is in the spirit of Omega, while the curving shape of the conference area is inspired by Swatch. The timber structure appears to be quite simple, but it is, in fact, rather complex. The conference hall structure is also in wood. Getting the correct amount of stability while accepting some variation given the sloping Swatch roof, was very difficult. The predictable deformation generated by the roof was a complicated element for the conference hall that had to be taken into account."

A view from the bridge that crosses over Rue Nicolas G. Hayek.

Shigeru Ban
makes wood
contemporary.

Shigeru Ban and his team have clearly helped contemporary timber construction to advance with the Cité du Temps. The innovations that they brought into the design, working with figures such as Hermann Blumer, will surely serve for other future buildings. Continuity in spirit and design was a priority for the team, from the CNC milling to the final signage used in the building. Yoshie Narimatsu recalls: "All holes in the timber structural elements were precut and assembled as much as possible in the factory. Each T-shaped girder was assembled in the factory. The curtain-wall façade is inspired by the spirit of Omega. There are radiant ceilings throughout which also serve an acoustic damping function. We collaborated with an internationally known Japanese graphic designer, called Kenya Hara, for the signage throughout the building. Dimensions, colors, font, and logo shapes were carefully designed to match the architectural concept of this building."

Contemporary Hybrid

More than for the Swatch Headquarters and the Omega Factory on the same campus, the word "hybrid" may best describe the Cité du Temps. It is a hybrid in terms of its own basic design, beginning with a concrete arch ground floor and the timber structure above. It is also a hybrid at the top of the building where a kind of UFO lands from across the street bringing with it the curves of the timber grid-shell roof. This hybrid character is, of course, related to Ban's own desire to link Swatch and Omega, but with it has come the challenge of integrating freer forms into what is basically a strict grid building. In fact, both the grid shell and oval conference roof and the stricter structure below are executed with the same sense of precision and quality. One grid meets the other in some sense and they bind together. Shigeru Ban had, of course, already completed an orthogonal timber and glass building for Tamedia in Zurich (see p.41) showing that wood and Modern(ism) could find a path together for the future. Where other architects have embraced the idea of unusual forms that are computer driven and shaped with steel, Shigeru Ban insists on the beauty of structure, on its transparency and visibility. An unexpected form in his hands has meaning in terms of its location and the overall program of the complex; it is not a gratuitous gesture, it makes sense. Looking deeply into his favorite material and forming it with the most advanced current production and building technology, Shigeru Ban makes wood contemporary. He conserves the warmth that wood offers and thus also makes contemporary architecture approachable and human rather than cold and distant.

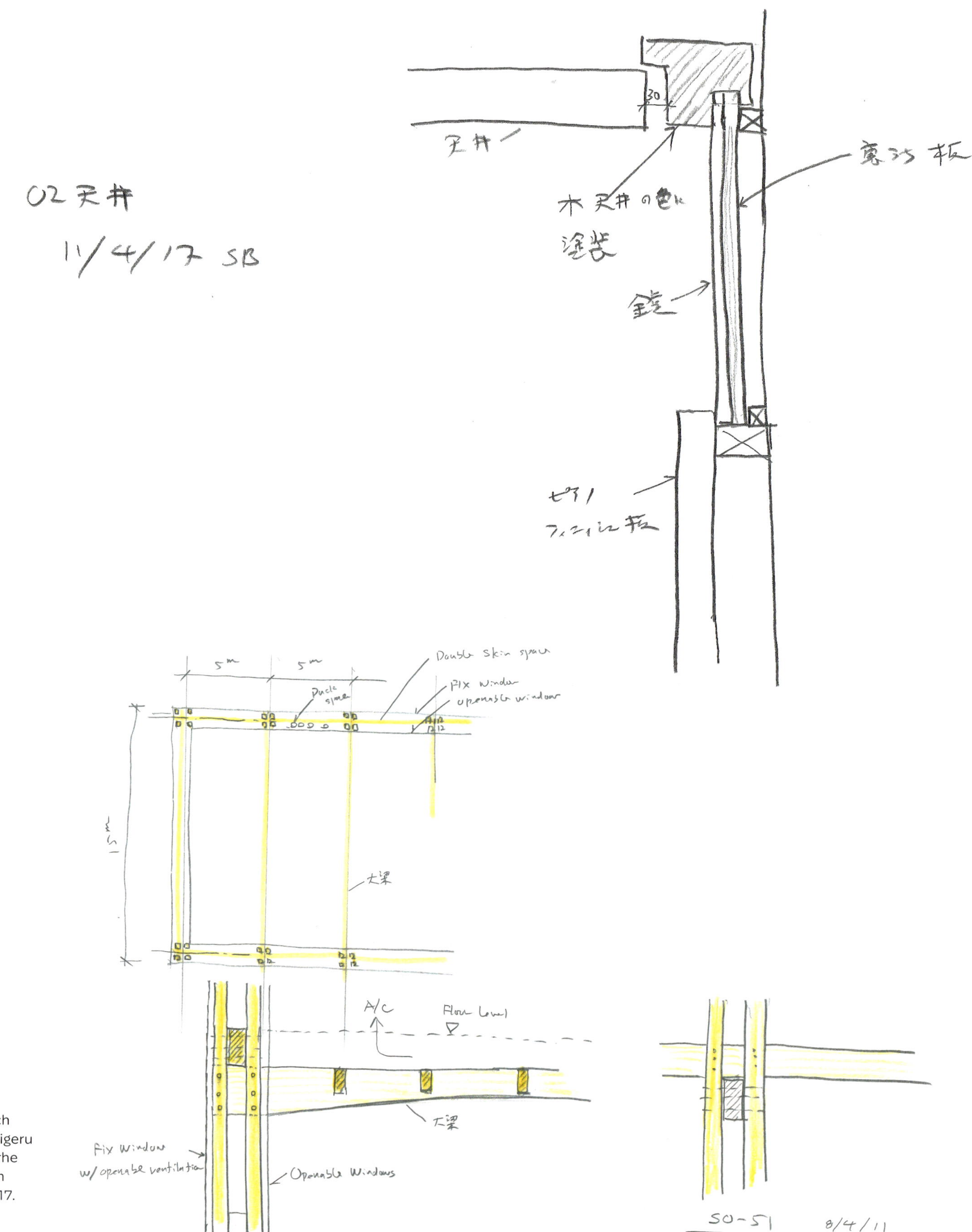

Top: a sketch made by Shigeru Ban during the construction phase in 2017.

Right: another sketch from the competition phase of the project.

Top: Shigeru Ban on site checking a full-scale timber prototype of the structure.

Right: the architect checking a ground-floor concrete arch of the Cité du Temps during construction.

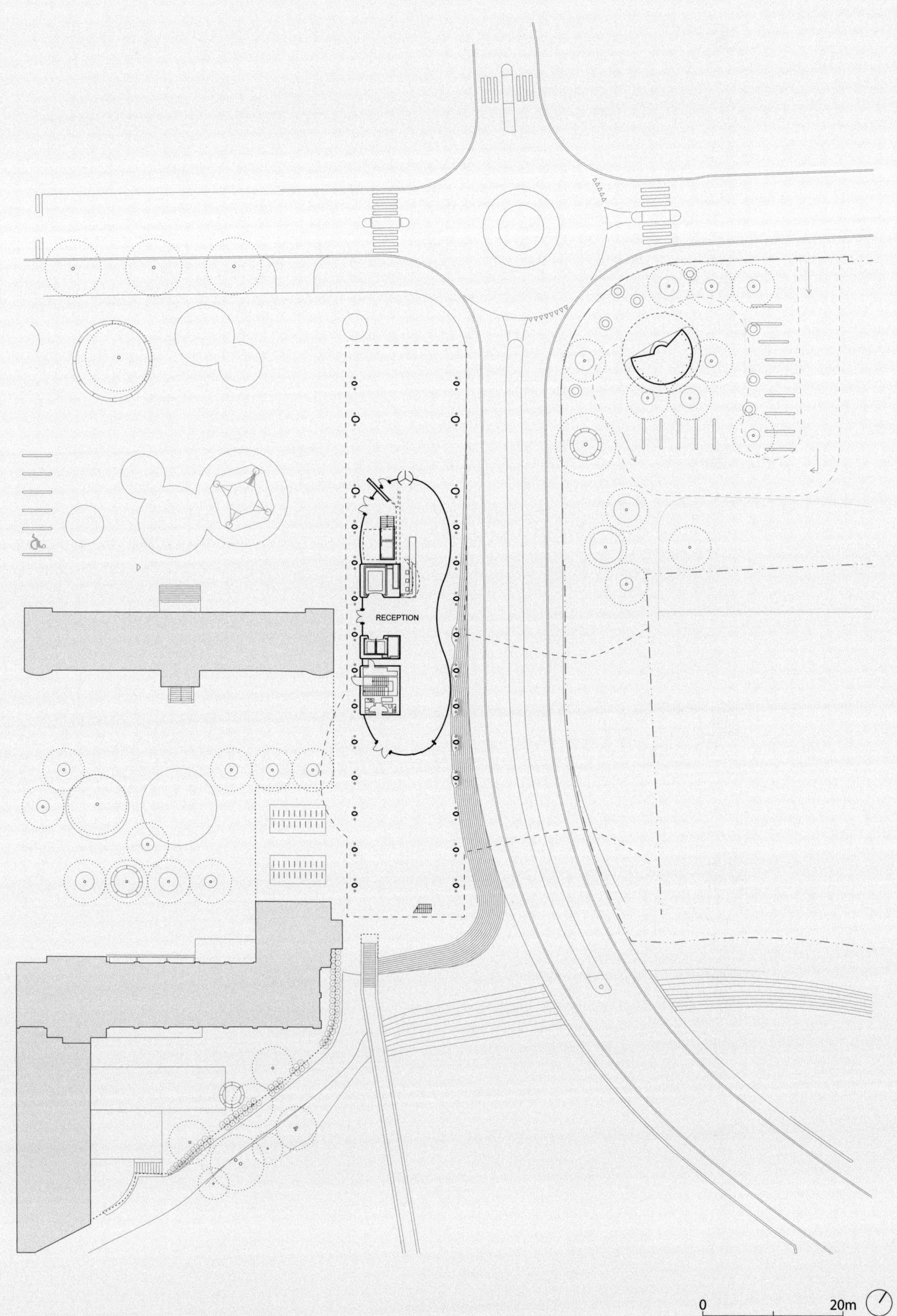

The ground-floor reception area of the Cité du Temps is visible in this drawing to the left of Rue Nicolas G. Hayek. The connection of the new building to existing elements of the Omega campus is evident as is the proximity to newly defined public spaces.

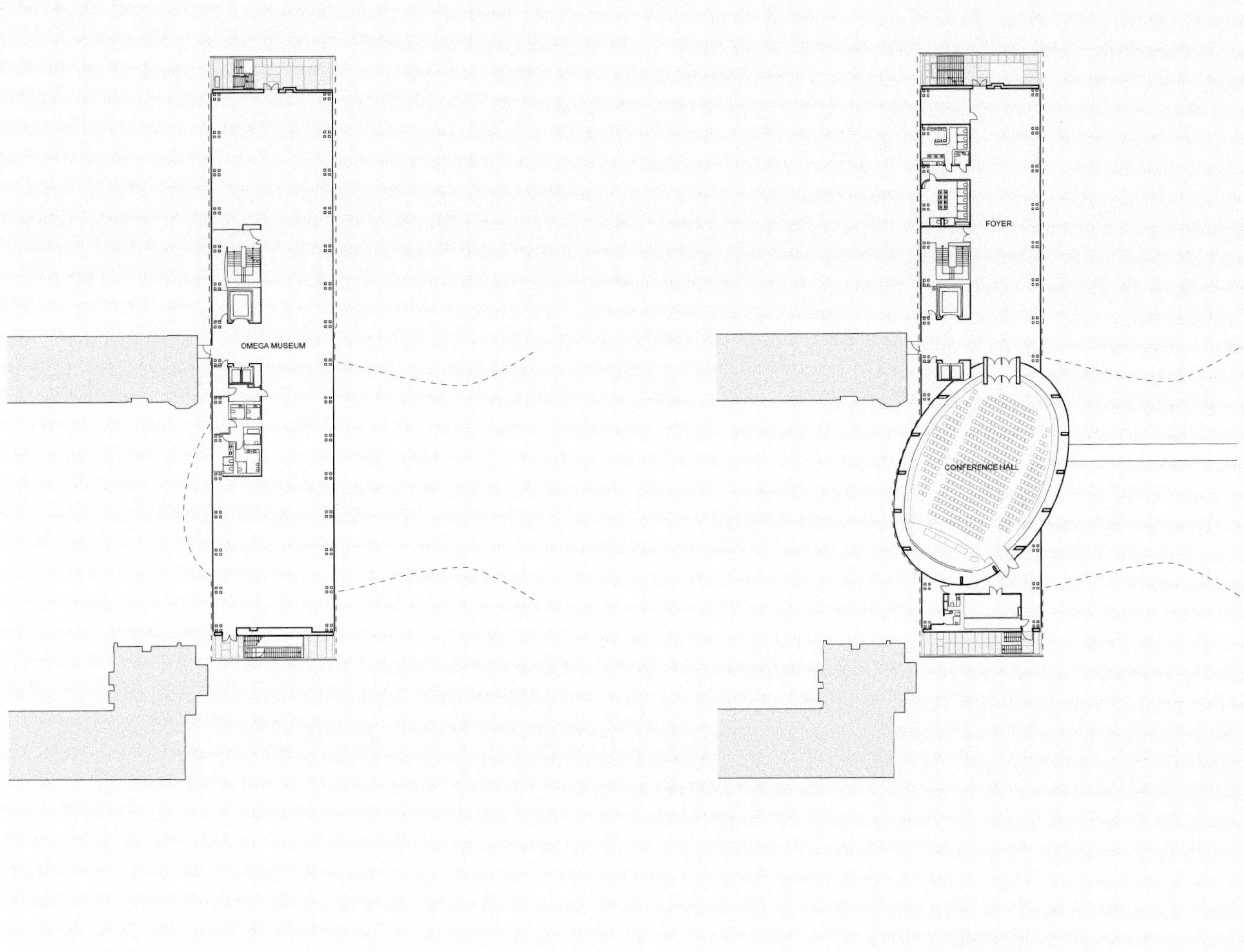

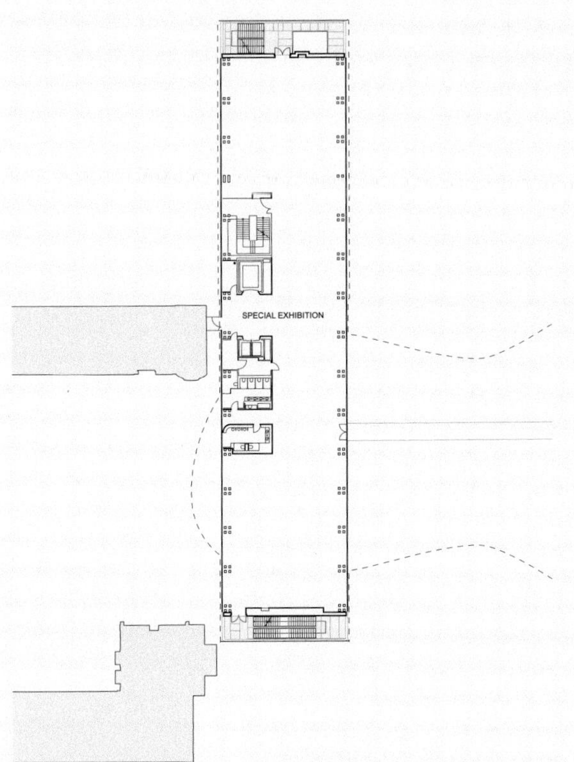

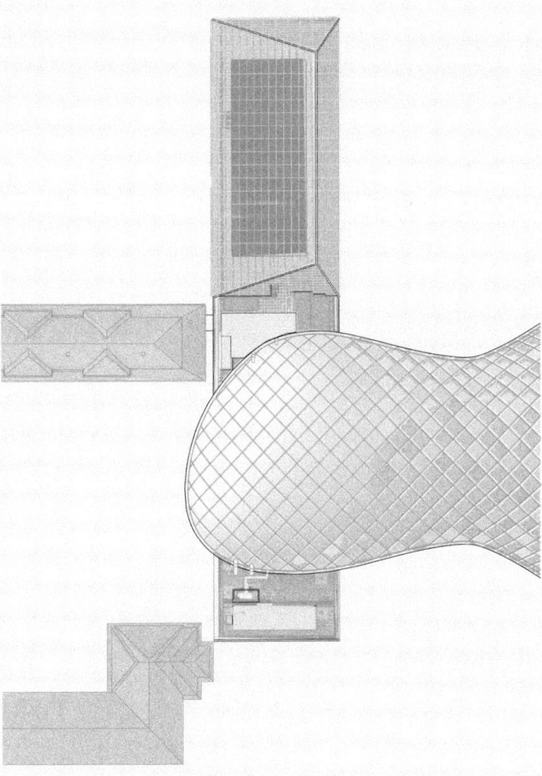

Plans of the Cité du Temps with the ground floor on the left page, the conference hall above, and the roof (left).

0 — 20m

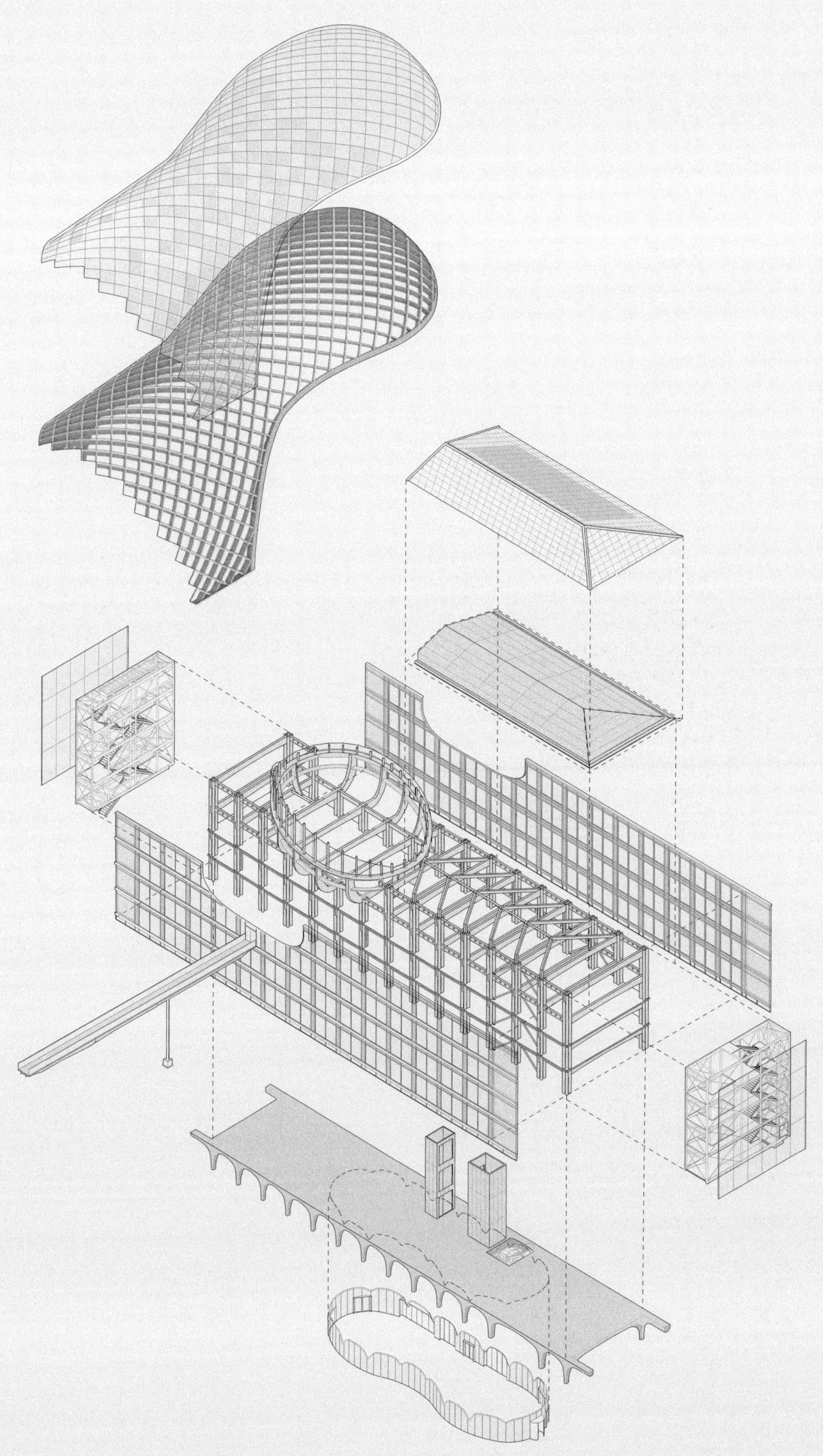

An exploded
axonometric
drawing shows
the different grid
and structural
elements of the
Cité du Temps.

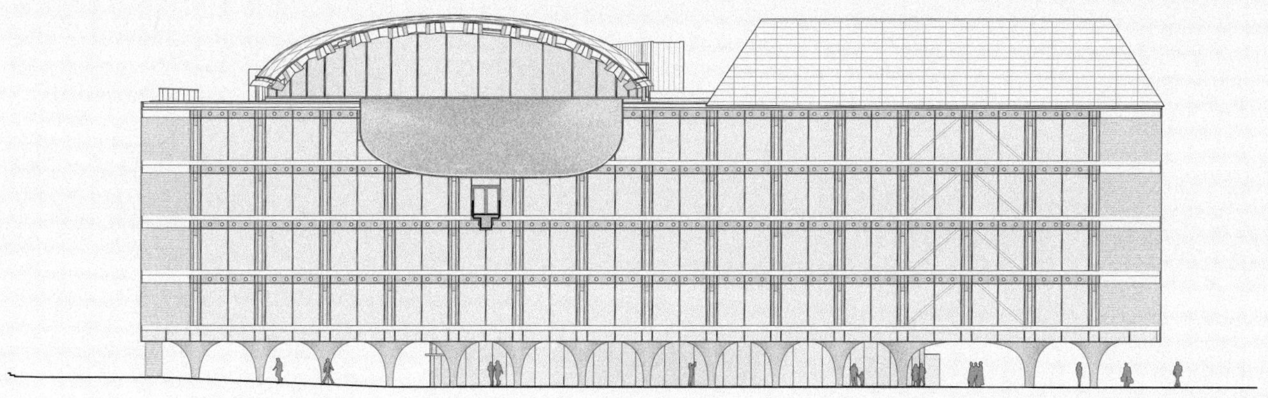

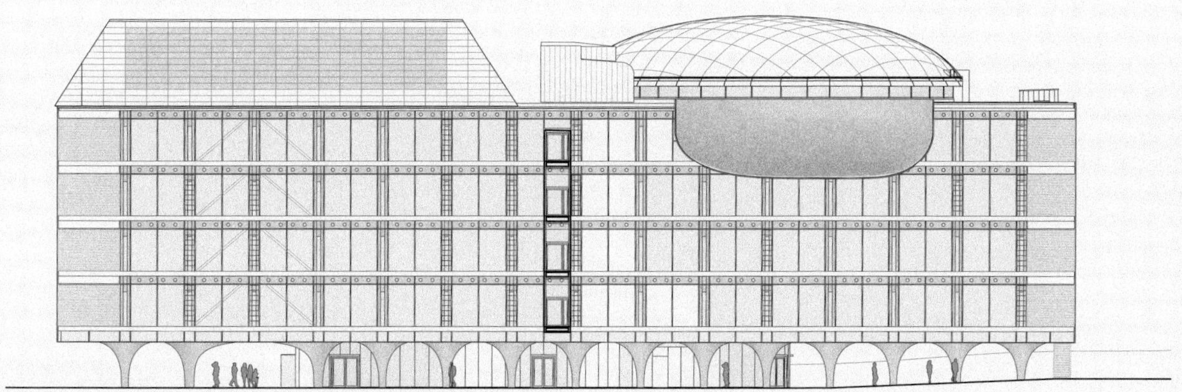

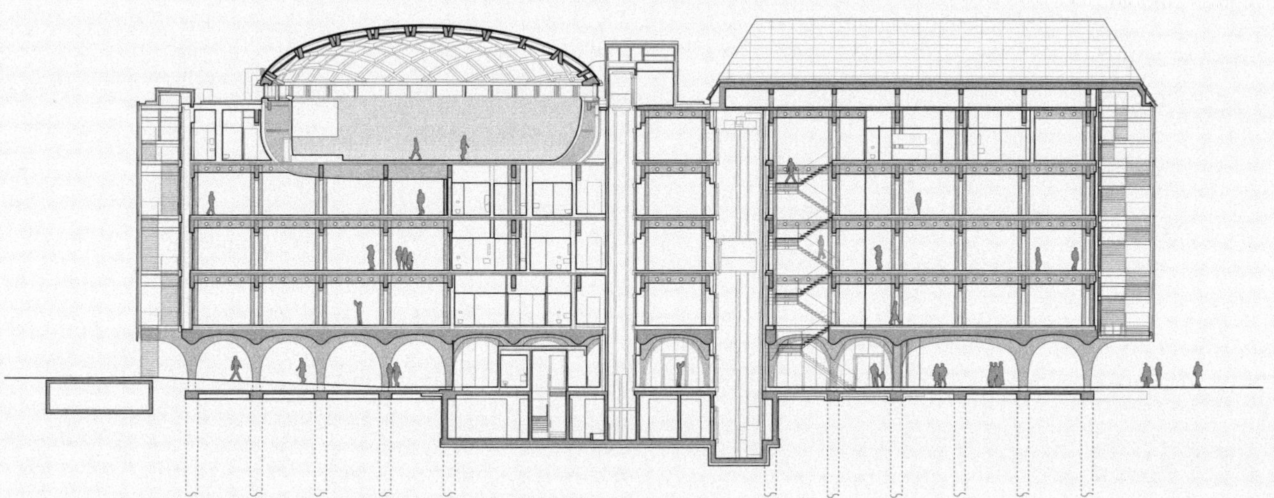

Two elevation drawings and a long section of the Cité du Temps with the conference hall at the roof level.

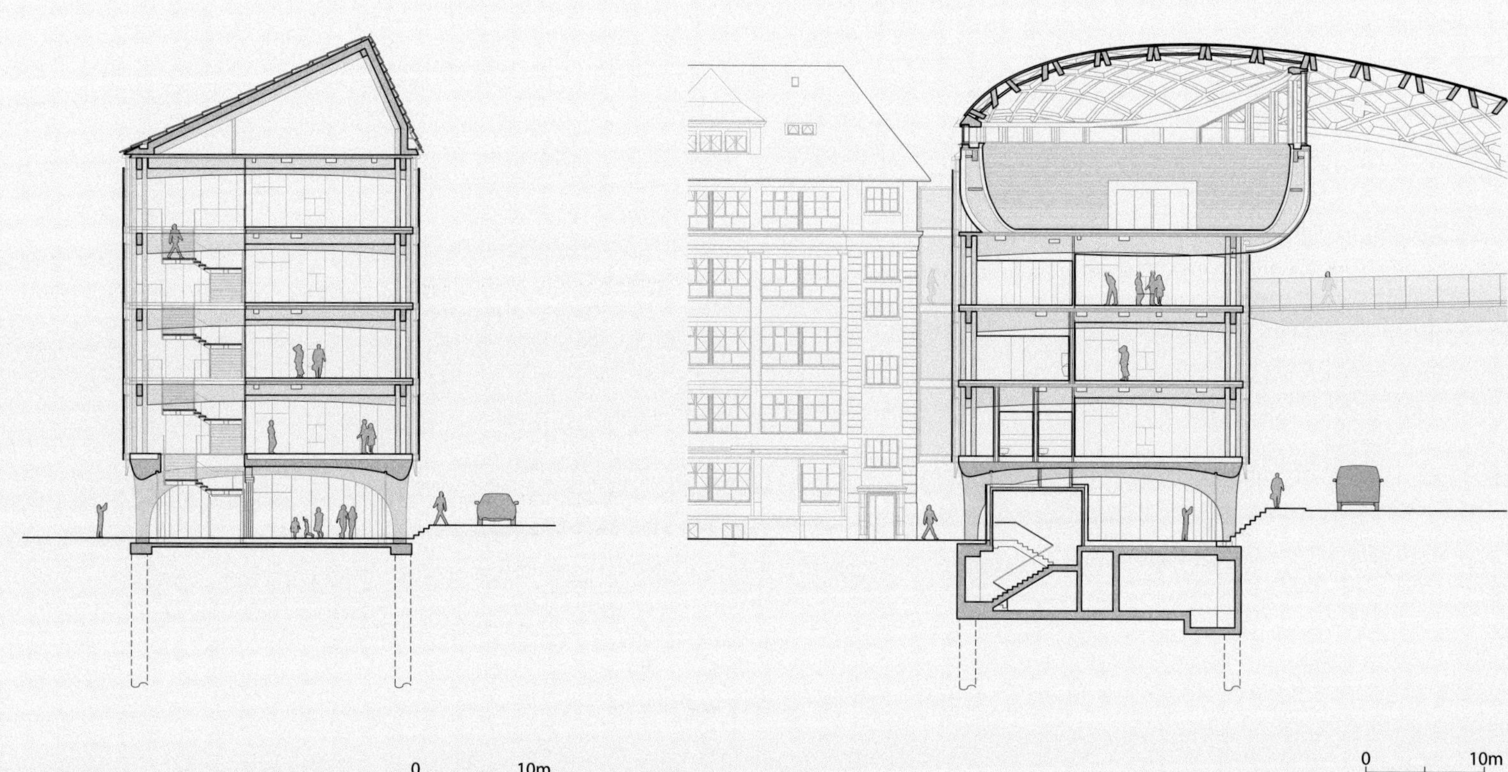

Cross sections
of the building,
with Rue Nicolas
G. Hayek on the
right, and the
upper conference
volume connecting
roof and bridge
seen in the right
drawing.

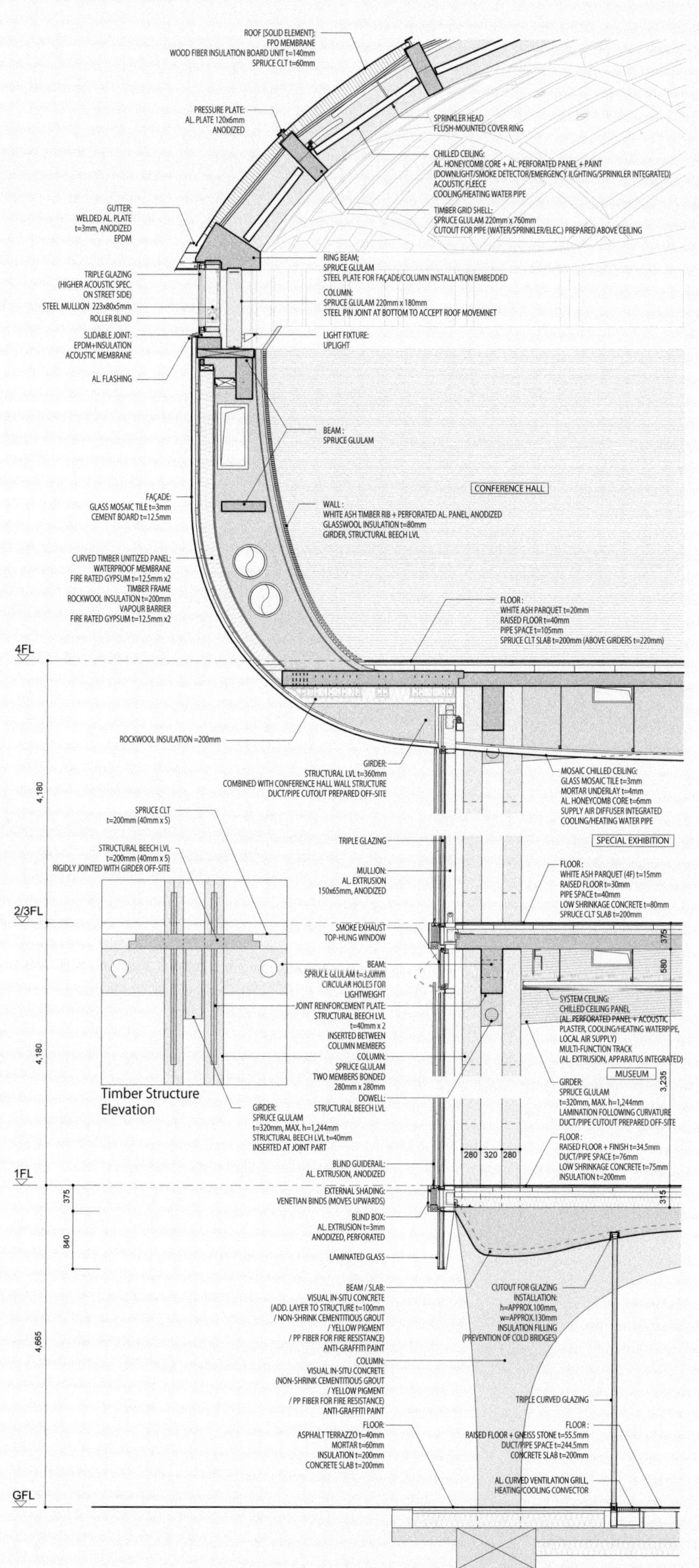

A detailed structural section drawing basically shows how the structure was put together using timber and concrete at the ground level.

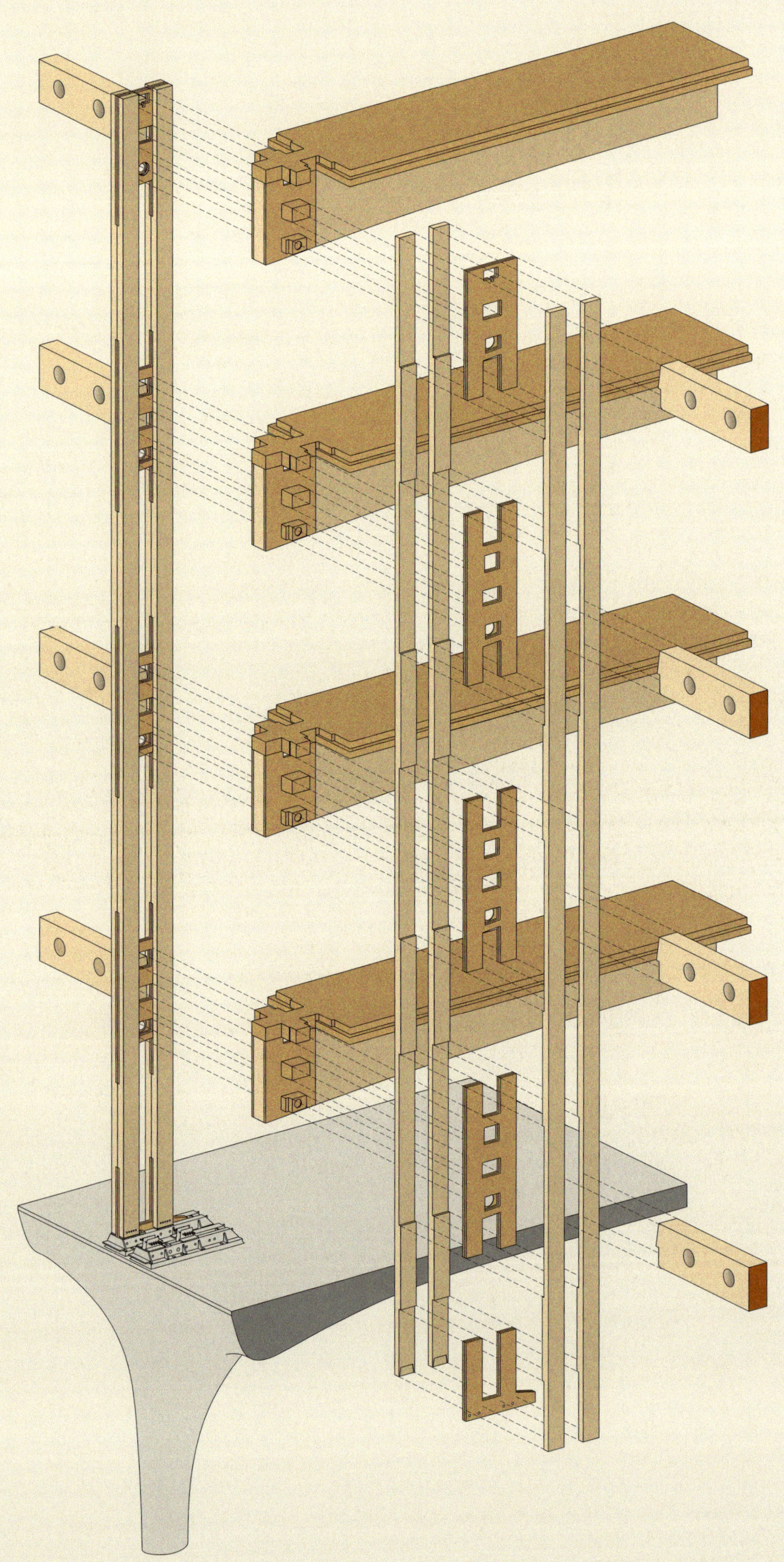

A timberstructure assembly diagram. Each 280-millimeter-square column is composed of two members. An H-shaped hardwood element is sandwiched between them strengthening the connection joint with the girders.

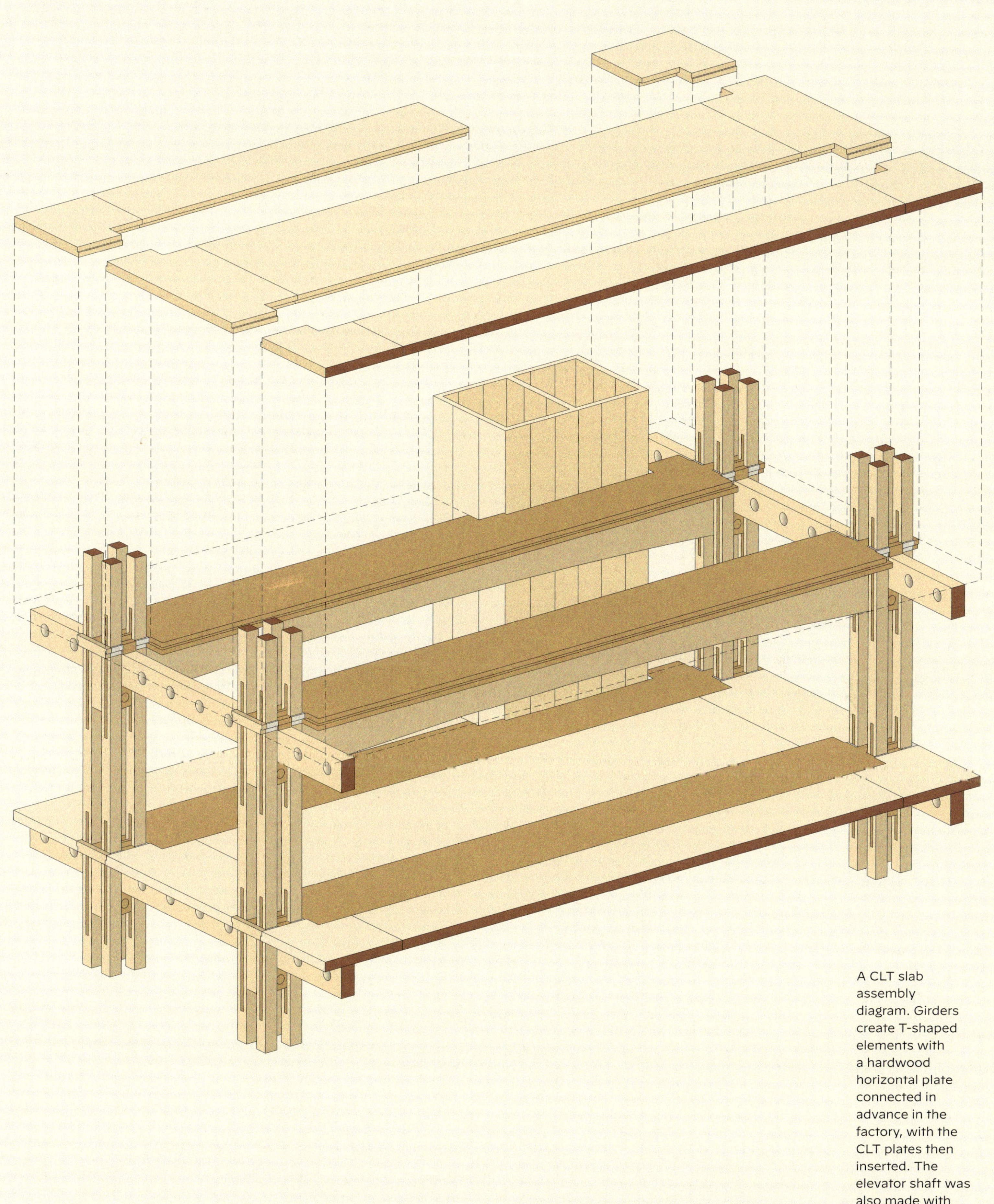

A CLT slab assembly diagram. Girders create T-shaped elements with a hardwood horizontal plate connected in advance in the factory, with the CLT plates then inserted. The elevator shaft was also made with CLT panels.

arti
Frutiger Frutiger
Blumer Lehmann

Previous double page: the timber-frame structure was built using a bespoke five-meter-wide scaffolding, which served as an assembly guide.

Above: the timber core for the elevator shaft was made with CLT panels and CLT floor slab plates.

Right page: a view up the staircase void. The connection between columns, girders, and beams is visible. The full-height timber-frame structure was installed on top of the concrete arches.

Above: the
ground-floor
concrete arches.
Yellow pigment
was mixed into
the cement to give
it a warmer color,
closer to that of
the upper-level
timber structure.
The cutout for
the curved glazing
was created with
formwork.

Right page:
construction of
the conference
hall. The bottom
of the bowl was
formed with
hardwood girders.
The grid-shell roof
was connected by
vertical columns,
whose bottom
detail allows
for a maximum
displacement of
80 millimeters.

Left: formwork for the ground-floor concrete arches. The surface of the formwork was repaired and repainted after several uses.

Above: work on the ground-floor concrete arches. A temporary roof moved together with the formwork to shield the concrete from sunlight and excessive temperature changes.

Following double page: the ground-floor reception area. The curved glazing creates an intimate and welcoming space. The marble staircase behind the reception counter leads up to the museum floors.

ZONE
30
CITÉ DU TEMPS

A view over the bridge between the Swatch Headquarters and the Cité du Temps. The oval conference center, together with the timber grid-shell roof, gives a unique character to the Cité du Temps and also connects it to the Swatch building.

Above: the north
pilotis on the
ground level,
with the Swatch
building visible in
the background.

Right page:
view from the
south side with
the stairs that
compensate for
the slope in the
street, creating
a different
atmosphere than
on the north side.

Left page: four
columns create a
rigid connection
by sandwiching
beams and girders
from two different
directions.

Above: a press
event held in the
conference hall for
the inauguration
on October 3,
2019.

The interior of the conference hall. The
timber grid-shell roof is covered on the
interior with timber ribs made of white
ash. Horizontal slits between each
rib serve as ventilation intakes at the
bottom and for acoustic absorption at
the top.

Above: the
exterior of the
conference hall
surface on the
fourth floor.
The mosaic tile
cladding of the
conference hall
bowl continues
from exterior to
interior.

Right page: the
east side of
the back of the
conference hall
on the fourth
floor. The Swatch
building is visible
through the glass
façade. Each
column is fitted
with floor lighting.

The 15-meter span of the open space
is created by the five-meter interval of
the timber-frame structure. The interior
solid walls are clad with lacquered MDF
panels.

Following double page: looking up the main staircase; the continuous full-height timber columns are visible. This structure was made possible by precise detailing, such as the required oversizing and joint details stipulated by fire regulations.

Left: the main
staircase at the
ground floor.
Lighter steel stairs
are used above
the level of the
concrete *pilotis*.

Right page: view
from the main
staircase. Activity
within the building
and the continuity
of the timber
structure are
visible from this
light staircase.

Interior view of the Swatch Museum on the third floor. Hydronic radiant heating and cooling functions from above the acoustic ceiling panels. Multi-function tracks placed every 2.5 meters allow lighting, sprinklers, or cameras to be attached in a flexible way.

Following double page: interior view of the Omega Museum on the first floor. It, too, has been fitted out to be a very flexible space. The design here is not the work of Shigeru Ban.

OMEGA FACTORY

The Omega Factory represents a sort of return to its point of origin for the Swiss watchmaker. Located on Rue Jakob-Stämpfli in the bilingual town of Biel/Bienne, where the company installed itself as Louis Brandt & Fils in 1882, the building has a floor area of 16,614 square meters on six levels plus a basement. The new structure combines all of the brand's assembly and testing processes under one roof. This consolidation of work means that the company's overall output will be more productive and dynamic than before. Watch assembly, watch bands, and packaging, together with the stock and logistics required for production, are now concentrated in the same building, as well as training facilities for the staff.

A Robotic Heart

There is a kind of big hole in the heart of the building that houses the automated storage system.

Although the main visible structure of the building is in timber and glass, this unusual structure has a concrete core that houses a fully automated storage and retrieval system on three floors at its center. The Central Stock contains boxes filled with all the necessary parts required for the brand's watchmaking. Visitors to the building can view the storage system and its robotic lifts in motion through specially built windows. The fact that only two highly trained persons are authorized to enter this dust-free space is a testimony to the unusual nature of the facility. Oxygen levels inside the storage and retrieval system are reduced to 15.2% as opposed to 21%, in order to guarantee that fires cannot start or spread. The Central Stock is 27.4 meters long, 9.4 meters wide, and 14.2 meters high. It uses two vertical lifts to move any of the 30,000 boxes for watch parts at four meters per second. It can complete 1,400 operations per hour delivering parts to the work benches of the watchmakers and returning boxes to their original locations.

A further example of the automation of the production is seen in the robotic arms and systems used to text Omega's Master Chronometer. They photograph, wind, shift, and spin the watches. Located on the third floor, the firm's METAS testing system also subjects the watches to magnetic fields of 15,000 gauss, or approximately the value found in a magnetic resonance imaging system (MRI). Watchmakers review the test results and ensure that every watch is correctly tuned and ready for sale. Robotic technology is used to identify and package the watches and also for laser engraving.

Keina Ishioka is a Director at Shigeru Ban Architects. She was responsible for the Omega Factory project and explains some of the factors that guided her work. She says: "Until this project, Omega did not have its own purpose-built factory. It has been fitting its production into existing buildings. So this was the first time it custom-made a building to be suitable to its watch production. It wished to have a centralized, numerically driven system to control the production." Ishioka explains that the Omega Factory is different from the Cité du Temps, for example, because it is built around the concrete core required for the automated storage system installed by the client. "There is a kind of big hole in the heart of the building that houses the automated storage system," she says. "All of the production materials that enter the building are put in this space. They can be delivered from there directly to the work benches of the watchmakers as required." Shigeru Ban often seeks to have elements of his buildings, or design decisions, fulfill more than one purpose, and that is the case of this concrete core which also houses stairs, elevators, and restrooms.

Three Priorities

Shigeru Ban emphasizes that his designs rely directly on the requirements that emerge from the site, the program, and his own priorities. In this case, Keina Ishioka explains: "There were three specific requests that shaped this project. The building had to be adaptable to be able to accept future changes in production methods. Omega was also very attentive to the health of the watchmakers who concentrate on very small parts in the artificially air-conditioned environment. This leads to specific body problems after hours of work, such as shoulder pains. Shigeru Ban also wished to integrate the requirements and philosophy of the Omega brand into the design—accuracy and a certain rigidity. This was translated with a fairly simple-looking structure." Ishioka imagines that "the automated production system is like an interior organ in the building. There is a visible timber structure in the work areas, but there are no columns or other interruptions within the spaces. This design responds to the client's request for adaptability in the future."

A watchmaking workshop. Each bench is equipped with an airflow system that reduces dust and cleans the air in the vicinity.

Following double page: the truck loading entrance of the building.

The spaces where the watchmakers work are enclosed in glass and specially ventilated to drastically reduce any potential sources of dust. The ventilation air flow required might have potentially created health problems for watchmakers after long hours of work. In order to carefully adjust air speed, Omega's ventilation system was tested during the planning phase and verified by a laboratory in Zug (Switzerland). Double columns rise up the full length of the façades of the fully glazed building every 5.4 meters. These columns are connected to beams that are anchored firmly in the concrete core with cylindrical beech dowels. The frictional resistance of the dowels creates the required stiffness in the frame, without the use of metal connecting parts. Floor slabs in the building are a wood-concrete composite, which serves to obviate any vibration, which must be avoided in the watchmaking process. The materials are chosen not according to any preordained architectural preference, but for reasons of efficiency and effectiveness. Wood is an integral part of the building structure, especially at the periphery, but the required concrete core is used to its best advantage.

A Dust-Free Environment

An ancillary function of the Omega Factory is to maintain contact with the public. Keina Ishioka explains: "Another particularity of the building is that it receives visitors or clients who are interested in seeing the workshop environment. The workshop is visible through the glass as is the central storage system. The visitor area is isolated from the work area both for reasons of security and because of the clean air environment required for watchmaking. The centrally located visitors' space is as modest as possible in order not to disturb the watchmakers."

Ishioka followed the entire construction process. She states: "The design was finished in 2013 and the construction was completed in 2017 on a fairly rapid schedule. We prepared the empty concrete box for the storage system with a very clean dust-free environment. The conveyor system goes in and out between the core and the workshop. Air-tight doors were required to avoid introducing dust into the storage system. That was done by a central storage system company. The dust control was a major planning issue inside the concrete box."

The materials are chosen not according to any preordained architectural preference, but for reasons of efficiency.

Like the original Omega buildings in Bienne, the building is located next to the Suze river. Hydropower was used to run early machines employed in watchmaking. Ishioka states: "The land near the river has a high water table, especially

Above: a view inside the automated
central storage system. The yellow
robotic frame runs along the corridor
between the shelves that store crates of
watch parts.

after the winter. This posed some difficulties during the excavation and construction below grade at the outset. However, this site-specific issue allowed us to better imagine the Omega brand, which has actually inherited the history of the watch industry and has continued to develop along the river."

Exemplary Sustainability

The Omega Factory project uses wood and concrete as its main structural elements. As Shigeru Ban insists, wood is a fully renewable construction material and though he may employ it more because of its limitations than because of its virtues, according to his own explanation, it is certainly to be considered an ecologically sound basis for contemporary construction. The Omega Factory goes much further in the area of sustainability; this is because of Swiss regulations but also because of the insistence of the client. The insulation standard chosen for the building exceeds the requirements of the Swiss building code. Efficient radiant heating and cooling is also used throughout. Excess heat from the production process is recovered and used to preheat the building's required hot water, while ventilation is carefully controlled according to the part of the workshops concerned. An aquifer thermal energy storage (ATES) system is used to inject and extract groundwater at a temperature between 10° and 16° centigrade, with a heat exchange system that employs radiant panels for cooling and controls winter temperatures with a heat pump. Further energy is obtained from photovoltaic panels located on the southeastern roof of the building. Micro-inverters installed behind the solar panels allow the system to directly produce AC current.

An Obvious Success

The rectangular building is 72 meters long, 34 meters wide, and 34 meters high. Its wooden structure is submitted to fewer constraints than that of the Cité du Temps, for example, because of the solidity of the required concrete core. This allows the design of the wood frame to be somewhat simpler and lighter than would be the case in an all-timber building. As seen from the outside, the Omega Factory is a rigorous grid-driven building with ample low-iron glazing that provides the unpolarized natural light, which is important for the quality control of precision watchmaking, and views of the exterior preferred for watchmaking. Other elements, such as the façade transom height, are determined by considerations related to the chariots used by the watchmakers, emphasizing the fact that the building has been carefully thought out to maximize its production potential. The façade profile itself is also custom-made, having a groove of 8 x 8 millimeters in which to insert a standard buffer rubber (D-profile) in order to protect the chariot in case it hits the façade. Such detailing, as well as the final aesthetics of the overall design, emerged during the many fruitful discussions with the client. The building is parallel to Rue Jakob-Stämpfli and is thus perpendicular to the Cité du Temps, which is located further to the east on the same campus. The western end of the Factory has an unusual detail. A required steel fire escape stairway is framed by two very large cone-shaped volumes that are used to provide air conditioning to each level. The air volume required was calculated by engineers and Shigeru Ban shaped the cones accordingly, covering the ducts with stainless steel. Like some other aspects of Shigeru Ban's architecture, this detail may appear a little "quirky" but is, in fact, generated from the facts of the project. According to Shigeru Ban: "Omega's main production building is designed to architecturally represent the philosophy of the brand. The structural system of the building is characterized in its rigid and formal column/beam timber frame with its wood joinery detail, expressing the accuracy and precision of Omega." To some extent, as he did for Tamedia in Zurich (see p.41), Shigeru Ban has created a rigorous modern building with a visible wood structure and a good deal of glass. The fact that this building has a very large concrete core is not visible from the outside, but it does simplify structural issues, making the required wood and its joinery somewhat easier to deal with, anchored as it is in concrete. Ban succeeds in relating his design to the rigor of the brand, one of his own major goals, and that of the client as well. The efficiency and attractiveness of the building are a testimony to the architect's successful resolution of another complex set of problems, this time based in the complexities of watchmaking. The new factory is at home in relation to the older buildings on the Omega campus at the same time as it projects a forward-looking, solid image.

> Ban succeeds in relating his design to the rigor of the brand, one of his own major goals, and that of the client as well.

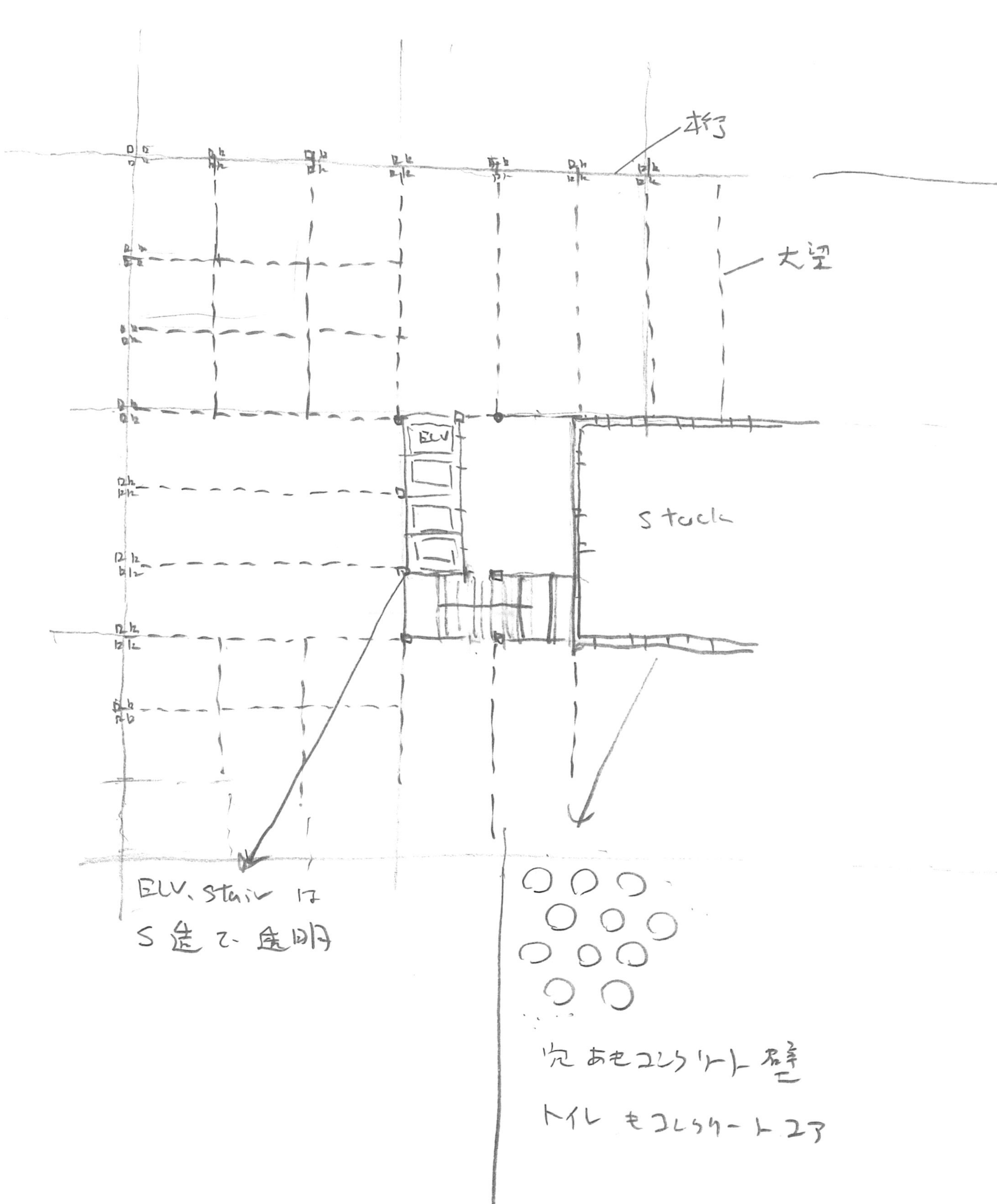
桁
大望
ELV
stock
ELV. stair は
S造で透明
穴あきコンクリート壁
トイレ もコンクリート ？

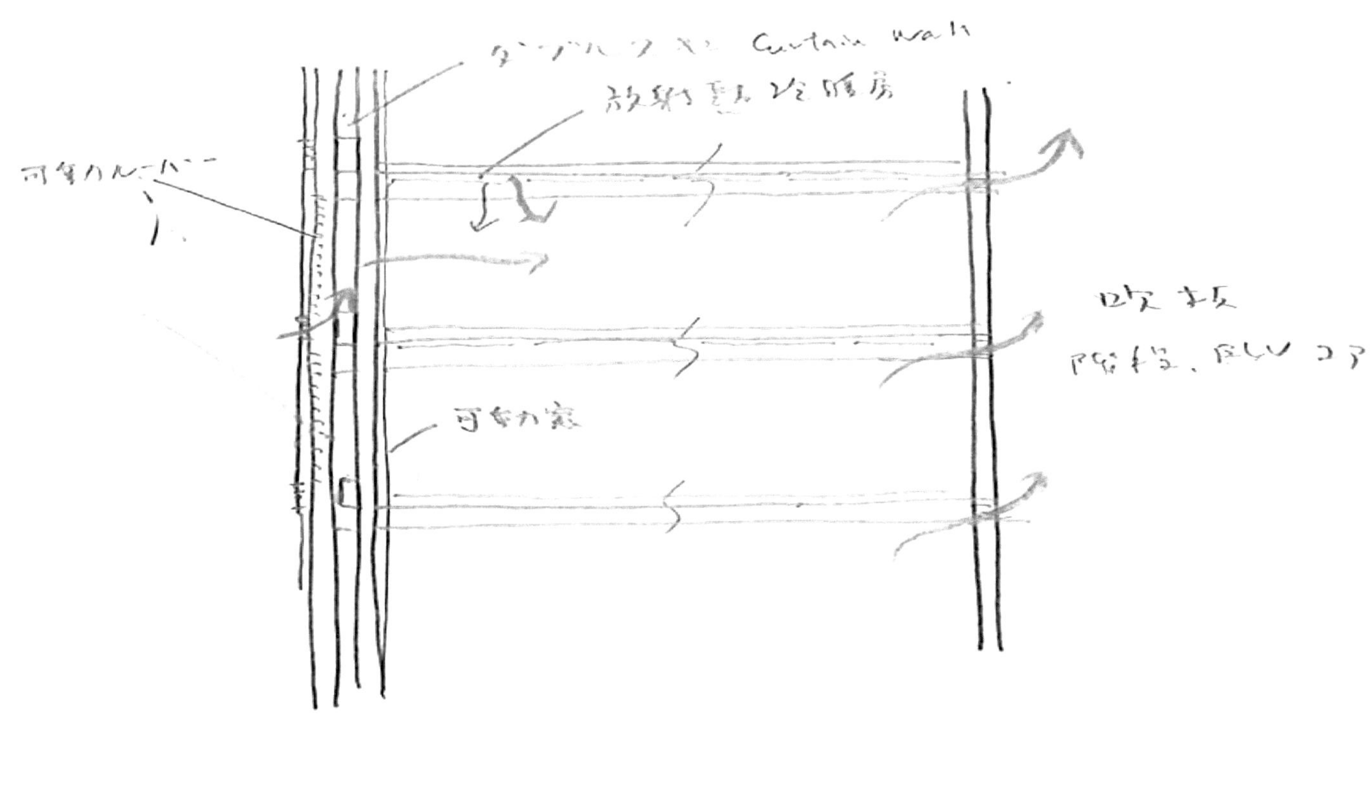

SO-51   15/4/11
O-O1 structure   S13

Sketches made
by Shigeru
Ban during the
competition
phase.

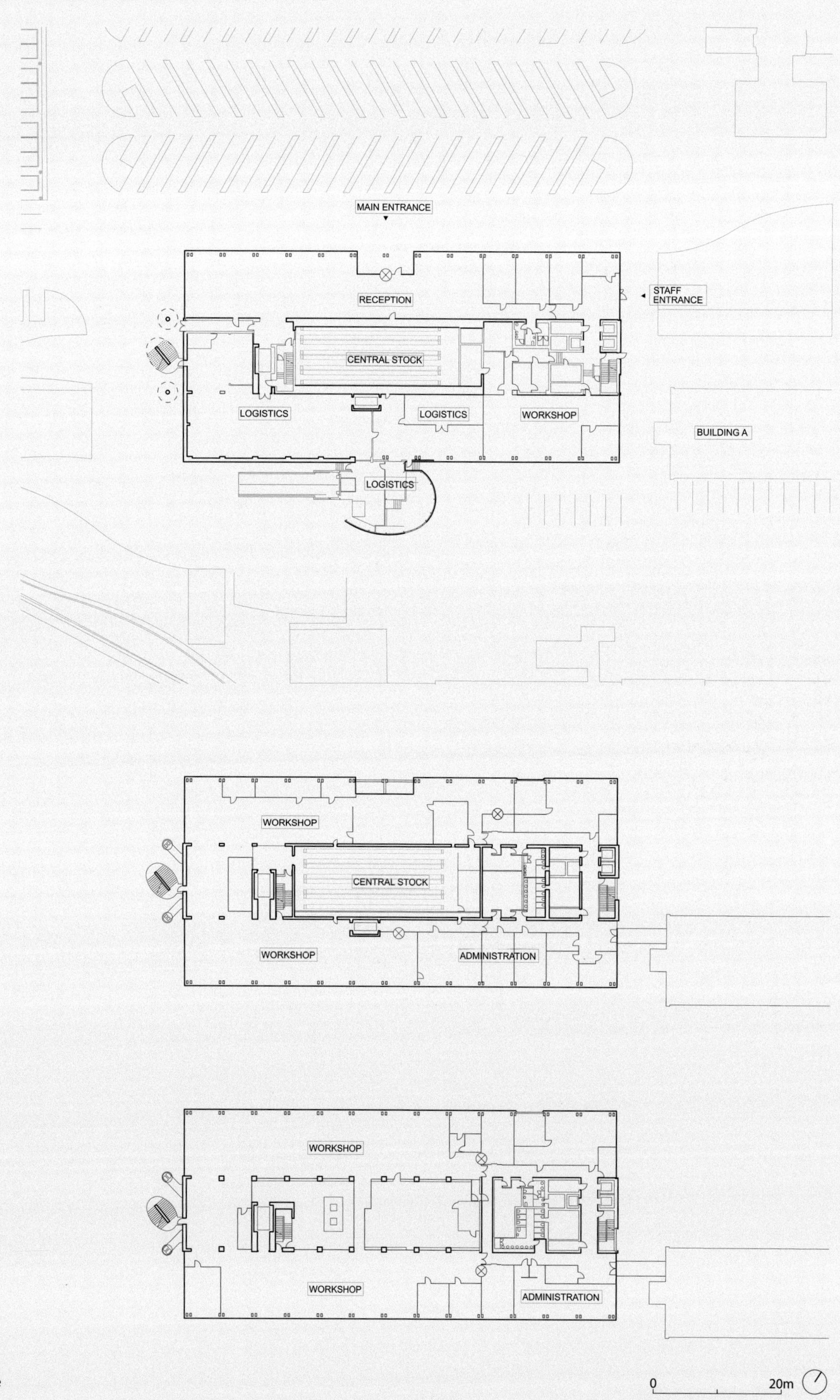

Plans of the
building with the
ground floor at the
top.

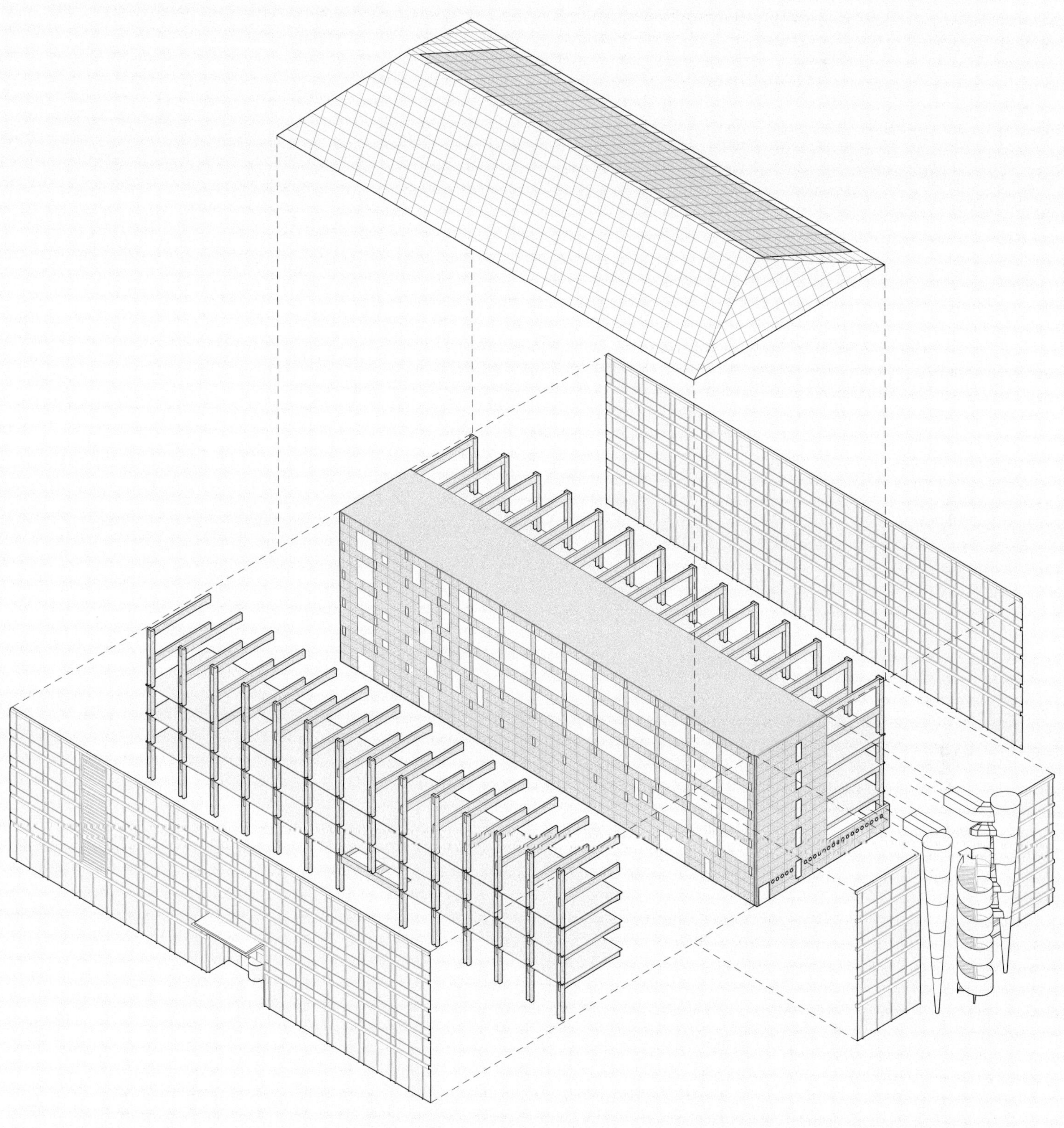

An exploded
axonometric
drawing of the
design and grid
system.

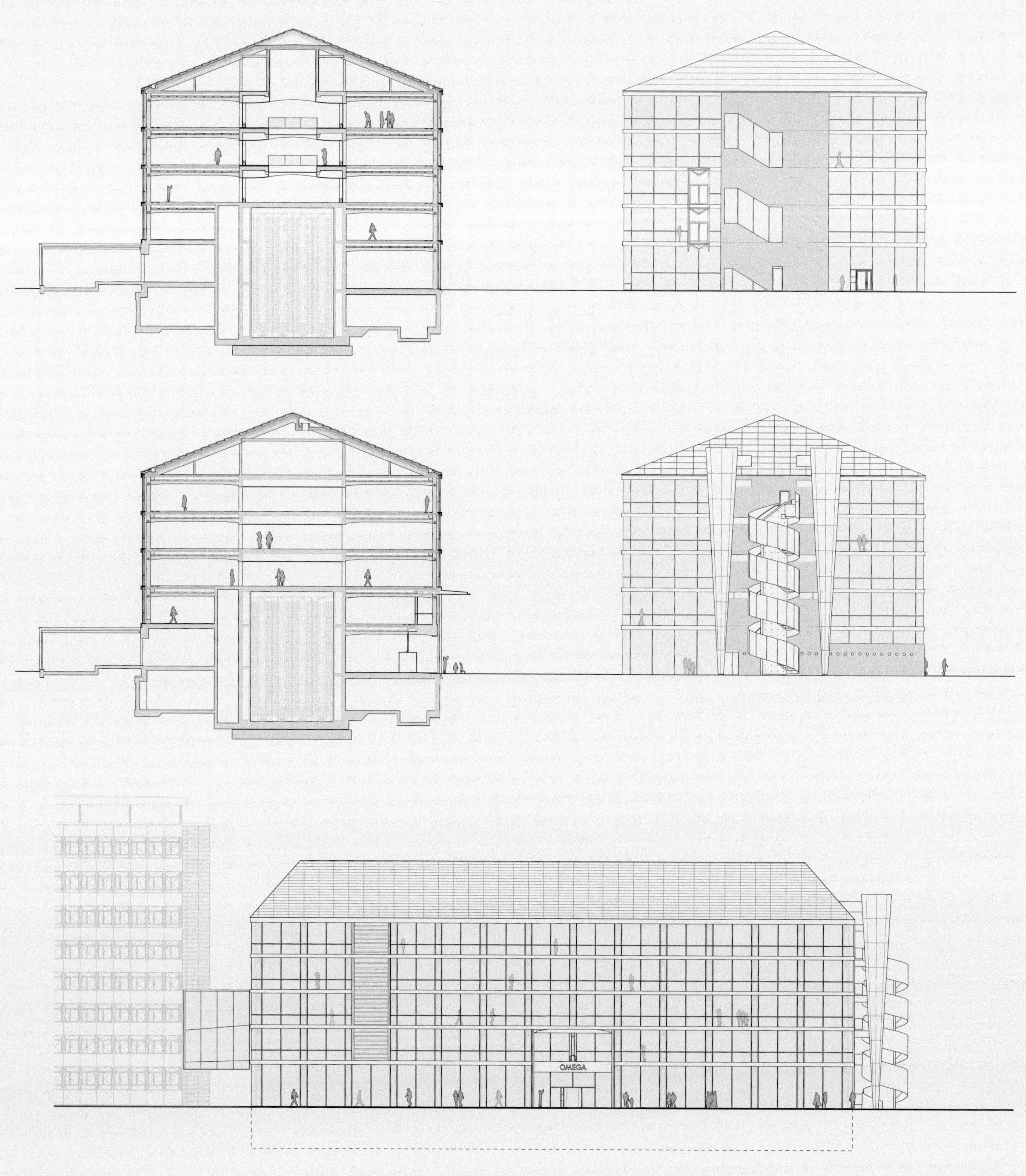

Cross section and
short elevation
drawings above
the entrance
elevation.

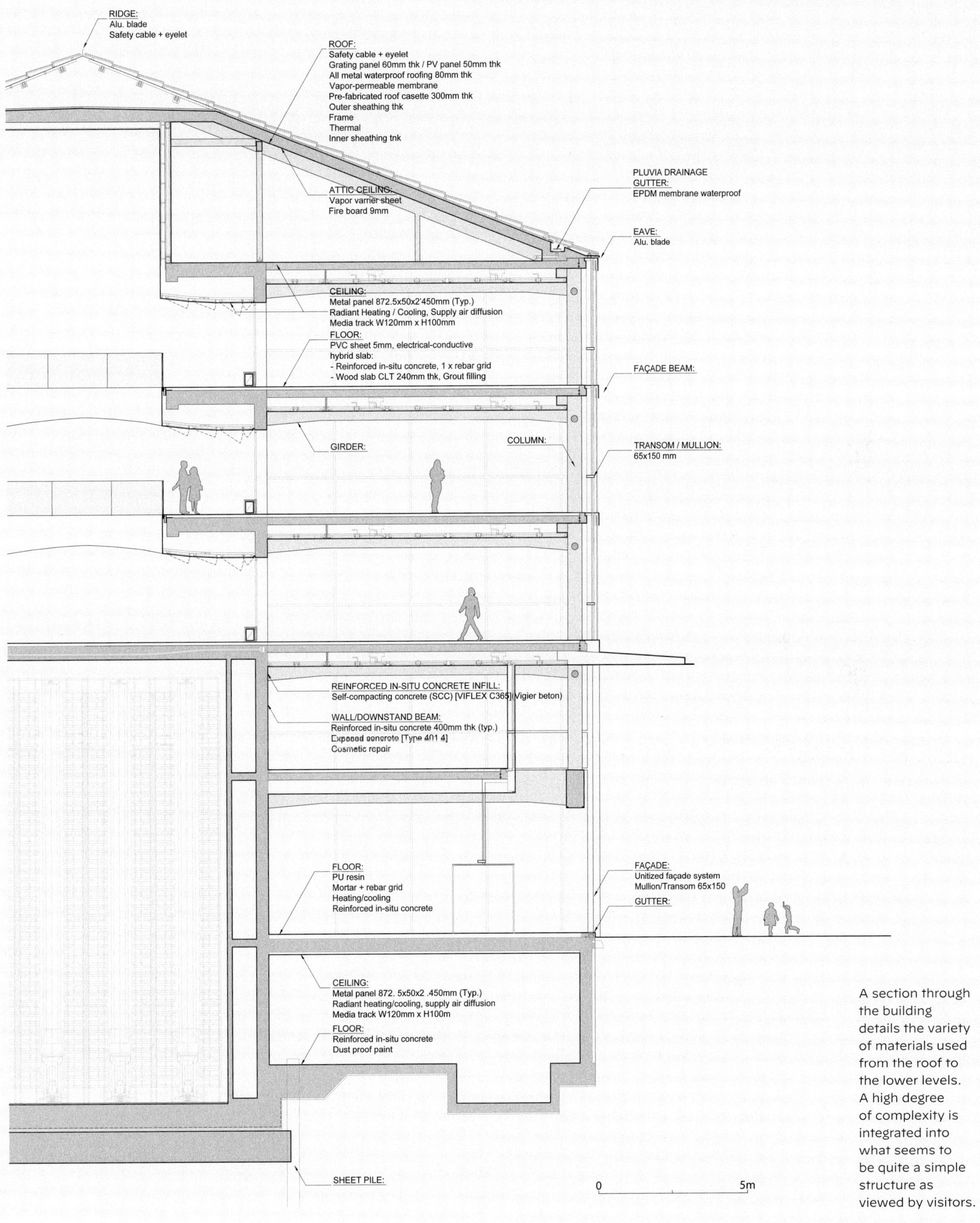

A section through the building details the variety of materials used from the roof to the lower levels. A high degree of complexity is integrated into what seems to be quite a simple structure as viewed by visitors.

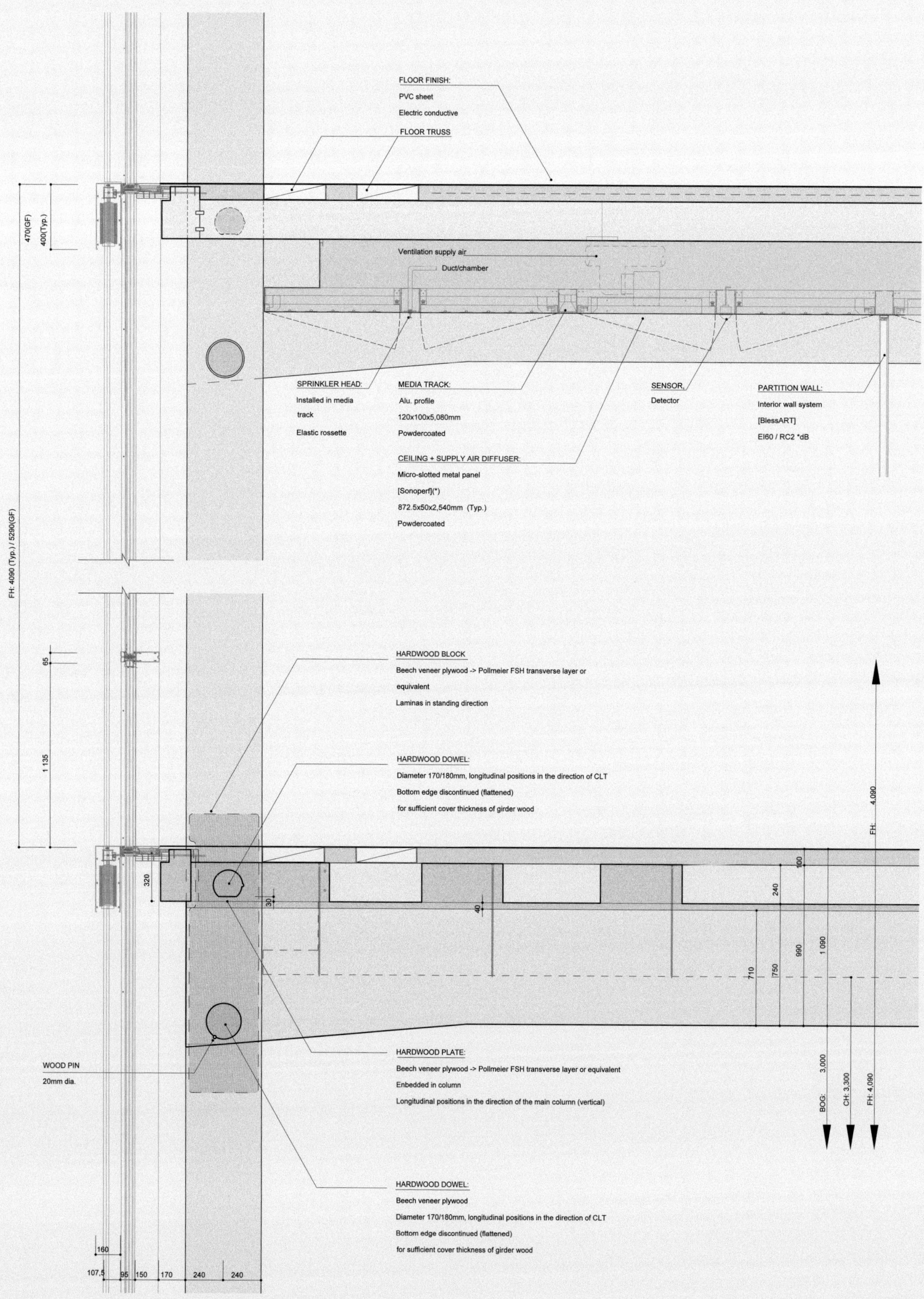

470(GF)
400(Typ.)
FH: 4.090 (Typ.) / 5290(GF)
65
1 135
320
WOOD PIN
20mm dia.
160
107,5
95
150
170
240
240

FLOOR FINISH:
PVC sheet
Electric conductive
FLOOR TRUSS

Ventilation supply air
Duct/chamber

SPRINKLER HEAD:
Installed in media
track
Elastic rossette

MEDIA TRACK:
Alu. profile
120x100x5,080mm
Powdercoated

CEILING + SUPPLY AIR DIFFUSER:
Micro-slotted metal panel
[Sonoperf](*)
872.5x50x2,540mm (Typ.)
Powdercoated

SENSOR,
Detector

PARTITION WALL:
Interior wall system
[BlessART]
EI60 / RC2 *dB

HARDWOOD BLOCK
Beech veneer plywood -> Pollmeier FSH transverse layer or
equivalent
Laminas in standing direction

HARDWOOD DOWEL:
Diameter 170/180mm, longitudinal positions in the direction of CLT
Bottom edge discontinued (flattened)
for sufficient cover thickness of girder wood

HARDWOOD PLATE:
Beech veneer plywood -> Pollmeier FSH transverse layer or equivalent
Enbedded in column
Longitudinal positions in the direction of the main column (vertical)

HARDWOOD DOWEL:
Beech veneer plywood
Diameter 170/180mm, longitudinal positions in the direction of CLT
Bottom edge discontinued (flattened)
for sufficient cover thickness of girder wood

FH: 4.090
100
240
710
750
990
1.090
BOG: 3.000
CH: 3.300
FH: 4.090

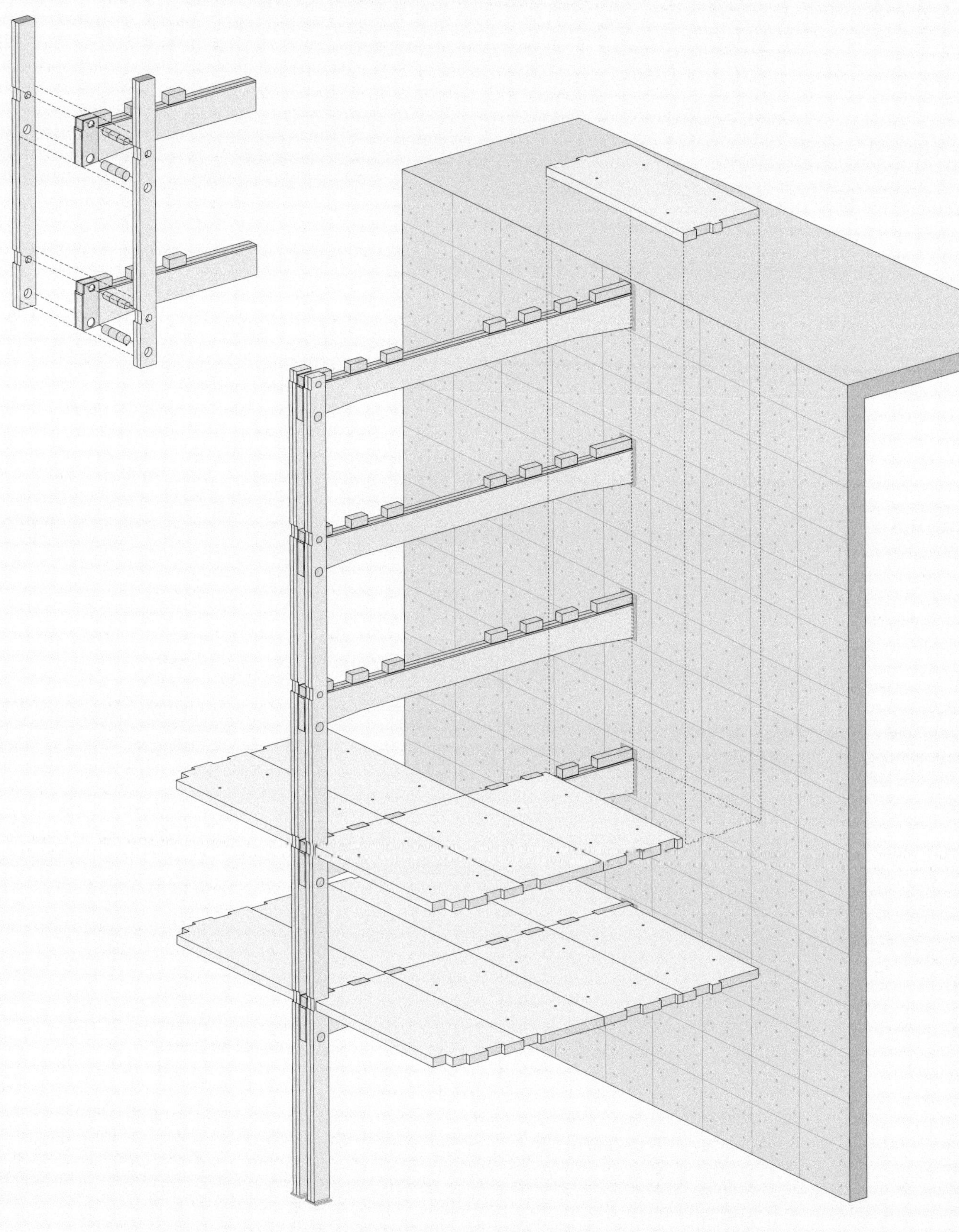

A detailed drawing of the structural system showing the hardwood blocks, dowels, and plates, together with other elements such as the ventilation ducts. In this instance the wooden structure is anchored in the concrete core used for the robotic retrieval system of the factory.

A mobile wooden
scaffolding
system called
the "Giraffe" was
custom-made for
the project and
moved from one
bay to the next,
guiding the timber
construction.

Following double
page: the wooden
structure was
created on either
side after the
completion of the
concrete core.

Top: the joinery
work connecting
a wooden beam
and slab.

Left (and right):
the installation of
a floor slab.

The construction
of the glazed
façade proceeded
in a cascading
manner after the
completion of the
wood structure.

Left page:
the horizontal stabilization of the building is maintained by the central concrete core. For the interface of the wood beams and the concrete, the end of the girder is jagged to increase the surface perpendicular to the support force at this point.

Above: a view of the column-less workshop space where all of the wood parts were prepared. The seams in the floor slab were inlaid with non-combustible material because of fire regulations.

Following double pages: two views of the building at nightfall showing first its remarkable transparency as seen from the street side, and then the unexpected metal air ducts and escape stairs on the narrow end of the rectangular plan.

OMEGA
OMEGA

A double-height break area with a glass shutter in the closed position.

The same space
with the shutters
open.

Close-up views of wood connections. For the joinery of the column and beam a set of two cylindrical dowels made of beech hardwood were used like drift pins. The lamination direction of the lower dowels was inclined to most effectively resist the node point that the moment acts on.

Above:
a view toward
a workshop
from the central
concrete core.

Right page:
a connecting
bridge between
the existing
workshops and
the new factory.

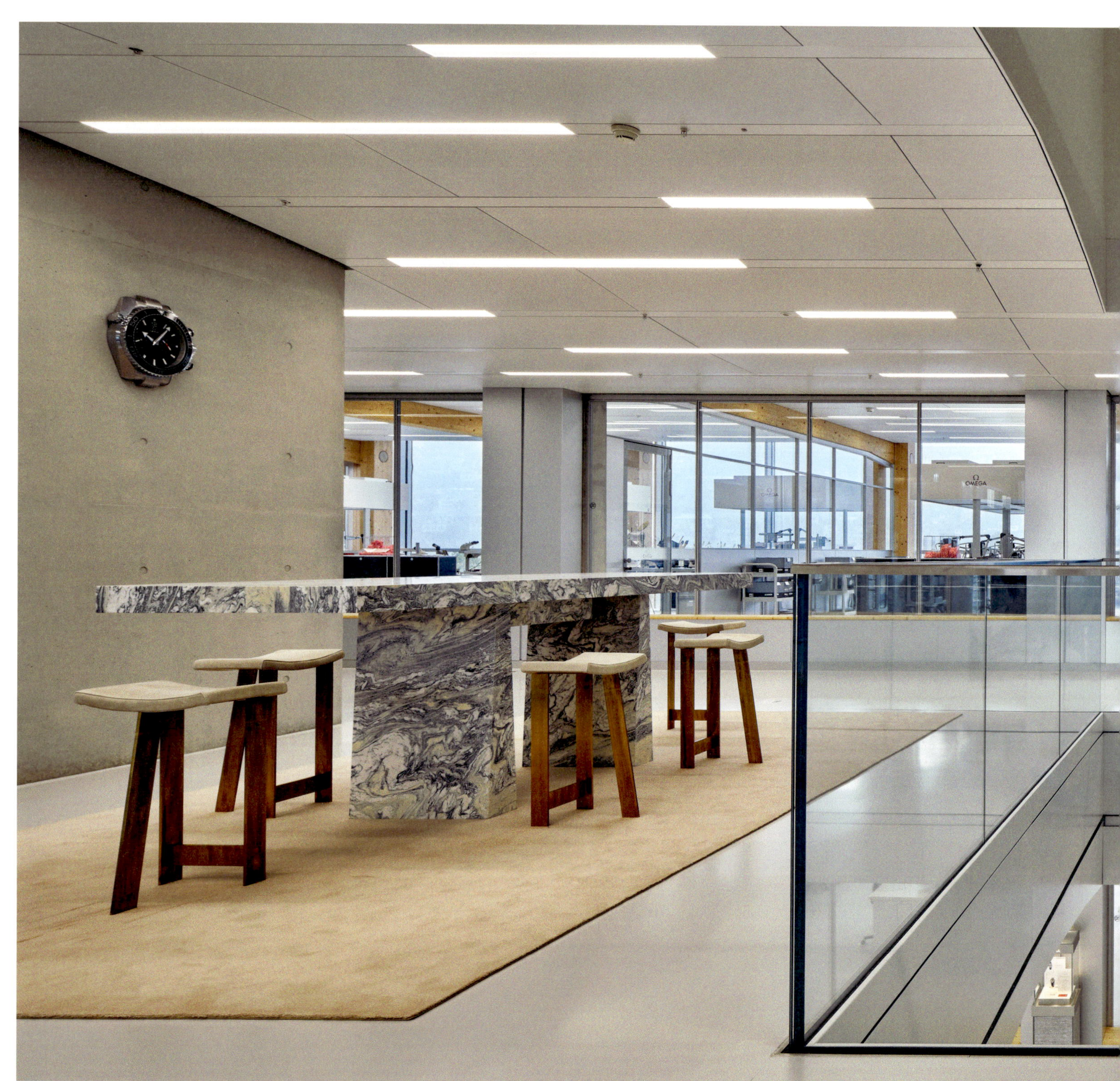

The visitor tour area is in the midst of
the large workshop floor, commanding
a view of the working space without
disturbing the process or posing a risk
for the required air cleanliness.

Above: the guest reception area at the start of the workshop tour, also used for Omega exhibitions and receptions.

Right page: the contrast between the existing workshop and the new factory.

Left page: the generosity of light and space generated by Shigeru Ban's design is clear in this picture of unoccupied space. A visual connection to the outside environment is also an important element for those who work here every day.

Above: in the same—now occupied— volume desks and other equipment clearly fill the space but the luminosity required for work and the relation to the exterior are still very much in evidence.

Above: a small
robotic system
that handles
finished watches
is located on the
first floor. Usually,
this type of
system is a closed
metal box but, to
match with the
design concept
of the building,
Shigeru Ban had
it customized
with transparent
cladding.

Right page: the
three-story central
storage system
located in the
center of the
Omega Factory
is equipped with
four robots that
manage 30,000
containers with
small parts and
components
that can be
delivered to the
watchmakers on
demand.

Seen down-river from the factory, the lower end of the Omega Factory is visible in the background. The image shows how the new architecture blends seamlessly into the urban environment while still providing a contemporary presence.

Credits for the Swatch Omega Campus

Shigeru Ban Architects

chronologically:

Omega Factory
Cité du Temps
Swatch Headquarters

Location:

Omega Factory: Jakob-Stämpfli-Strasse 96, 2502 Biel/Bienne, Switzerland
Cité du Temps: Nicolas G. Hayek Strasse 2, 2502 Biel/Bienne, Switzerland
Swatch Headquarters: Nicolas G. Hayek Strasse 1, 2502 Biel/Bienne, Switzerland

Design period:

Omega Factory: December 2011–September 2013
Cité du Temps: December 2011–November 2014
Swatch Headquarters: December 2011–November 2014

Construction period:

Omega Factory: October 2013–February 2017
Cité du Temps: December 2014–September 2019
Swatch Headquarters: December 2014–October 2019

Gross square meters:

Omega Factory: 16,614.00 m²
Cité du Temps: 7,061 m²
Swatch Headquarters: 25,016 m²

Client:

Omega Factory: Omega Ltd.
Cité du Temps: The Swatch Group Ltd.
Swatch Headquarters: Swatch Ltd.

CREDITS

Architect:

Shigeru Ban Architects Europe
6 rue de Braque, Paris, France
+33 (0)1 70 71 20 50
http://www.shigerubanarchitects.com/

Shigeru Ban, Overall Design Lead
Taro Okabe, Overall Project Lead

Omega Factory:
Keina Ishioka, Project Chief
Barbora Ngaboyamahina, Assistant Architect
Clio Dimofski, Assistant Architect
Maria Giulia Rotunno, Assistant Architect
Guillermo Gonzalez, Assistant Architect
Chika Tatsuta, Assistant Architect

Cité du Temps:
Yoshie Narimatsu, Project Chief
Conor Horgan, Assistant Architect
Akihiko Tanigaito, Assistant Architect
Philippe Sim, Assistant Architect
Kiyo Komurai, Assistant Architect
Natsuka Muto, Assistant Architect
Roberto Sini, Assistant Architect
Min Tang, Assistant Architect

Swatch Headquarters:
Taro Okabe, Project Chief
Jonas Epper, Deputy Project Chief
Matthieu Gabay, Assistant Architect
Takeshi Mitsuda, Assistant Architect
Takayuki Ishikawa, Assistant Architect
Maya Utsunomiya, Assistant Architect
Veronica Arianna, Assistant Architect
Emilie Bonzi, Assistant Architect
Michela Falcone, Assistant Architect
Marc Ferrand, Interior and Product Designer
Alessandro Boldrini, Assistant Architect
Chika Tatsuta, Assistant Architect
Clotilde Varinot, Assistant Architect

Local Architect (Competition and Concept Design):

Blaser Architekten
Austrasse 24, 4051 Basel
+41 61 278 95 55
https://blaserarchitekten.ch/

Cristian Blaser, Overall Project Lead

Local Architect (from Schematic Design through Site Supervision):

Itten+Brechbühl
Güterstrasse 133, 4053 Basel
+41 61 556 07 00
https://www.ittenbrechbuehl.ch/en

Jan Stöcker, Overall Project Lead

Omega Factory:
Andreas Stöcklin, Project Chief
Jacqueline Götschy, Assistant Architect
Alexander Kriegelsteiner, Assistant Architect
Anca Maria Jianu, Assistant Architect

Cité du Temps:
Christian Frischknecht, Project Chief
Anca Maria Jianu, Assistant Architect
Detmar Kleiner, Assistant Architect
Sergio Gil López, Chief Construction Manager
Feim Hoti, Deputy Chief Construction Manager

Swatch Headquarters:
Carolin Schaal, Project Chief
Christian Furter, Deputy Project Chief
Thomas Hottner, Assistant Architect
Takayuki Ishikawa, Assistant Architect
Sergio Gil Lopez, Chief Construction Manager
Oliver Lehmann, Deputy Chief Construction Manager
Marco Kämpfer, Assistant Construction Manager

Interior Design:

Shigeru Ban Architects Europe

Project Manager / Owner's Representative
Overall Project Management:

Hayek Engineering AG | Nils Kröger
Omega Factory:
Swatch Group Services Real Estate Development | Antoine Rembault
Cité du Temps:
Hayek Engineering AG | Thomas Huber
Swatch Headquarters:
Hayek Engineering AG | Niels Knandel, Pillar Martinez

Engineers:

Structural (wood, steel):
Création Holz
SJB Kempter Fitze

Structural (concrete, steel):
Schnetzer Puskas Ingenieure

HVAC, Sanitary, Building Automation:

Omega Factory:
Gruner
Gruner Kiwi
Roschi+Partners

Cité du Temps:
Gruner Roschi
Roschi+Partner
Gruner Kiwi

Swatch Headquarters:
Gruner Gruneko
ISP und Partner

Electrical:

HKG Engineering

Security:

Cité du Temps:
HKG Consulting
Hügli
Omega Factory:
HKG Consulting
Hügli
Swatch Headquarters:
Hügli

PV System:

BE netz

Network:

The Swatch Group Services

Façade Engineering:

Leicht

**Parametric 3D
(Cité du Temps, Swatch Headquarters):**

Design - to - Production

Energy:

Transsolar Energietechnik

Building Physics:

CSD Ingenieure

Fire/Safety:

BDS Security Design

Lighting:

Reflexion

Infrastructure:

WAM

Landscape:

Fontana Landschaftsarchitektur

Acoustics:

Commins Acoustics Workshop
Kuster + Partner

Audio/Visual:

Intelliconcept

Contractors

Omega Factory:
Project Manager: Swatch Group Services
Real Estate Development | Antoine
Rembault
Supervision: Itten + Brechbühl AG,
Switzerland | Pascal Diehl, Eric
Kopfhammer, Stefan Hoppe, Helmut
Kreuzer
Demolition: Kopp Robert
Scaffolding: Gatti
Site Safety: Securitas
Preparation Work: Alpiq InTec West,
ElektroPro & Flückiger Electricité, De
Luca , Kopp Ropert
Excavation: ARGE De Luca & Kopp
Concrete: De Luca
Micropile: Marti Bern
Timber: Blumer-Lehmann
Façade: Sottas
Loading: Morand R. et Fils SA, Meier
Systems
Glass Shutter: Aepli Metallbau
Fire Wall: AGI Bern
Roof: S+T fassaden GMBH, Sigi-
Gebäudehülle
Exterior Riser, Staircase: Bartholet
DECT: Fischer Electric
Electrical: Etavis Jag Jakob
Fire Alarm System: Siemens Schweiz
Smoke Exhaust Monitoring: JOMOS
Feuerschutz
Building Automation: MST
Systemtechnik, PentaControl
Switch Board: ElektroPro
UPS, Battery: ABB Schweiz
Heat Source System: RIEDO Clima

Düdingen
Ground Water Well: Marti Forster, Josef
Muff
Air Conditioning System: ENGIE Services
Compressed/Vacuum Air System: Jean
Reusse, Air Comprimé , Gardner Denver
Schweiz, Kaeser Kompressoren
Sprinkler: Oeschger Brandschutz
Lift: EMCH Aufzüge
Lift: Schindler Aufzüge
Palet Lift: Gilgen Logistics
Central Stockage System: Stöcklin
Logistics, Kardex Systems
PVsystem: Megasol Energie, Belenos
Clean Power Holding, EES Jäggi-Bigler
Oxygen Reduction System: Messer
Schweiz
Lighting: Zumtobel Licht,
Regent Beleuchtungskörper, SE
Lightmanagement, RS Licht nach Mass,
ERCO Lighting
LED Power Supply: Tic Beleuchtungen
Thermal Insulation: WUDEMA
Fire Insulation: Aare Dämmungen Bern
Dry Wall: Merazzi & Partner, MS Protect
Metal Substructure: D fischer Die
Metallbauwerkstatt
Metal Work: Herren, Mügeli Metalltechnik
Fire Shutter: Wolfisberg Tor-Technik,
Stawin
Interior Door: RWD Schlatter
Interior Wall System: BlessArt
Raumsysteme
Hybrid Slab Concrete: Effi Bau
Wood Fire Slab: SCHWAB-SYSTEM,
John Schwab
Interior Finish: HKM (PVC sheet,
parquet), B&L Bodensysteme (PU resin),
Pacitto Baukeramik (ceramic tile), Walo
Bertschinger (asphalt terrazzo), Wibatec
(carpet), AGB Bautechnik (raised floor)
Ceiling System: KST
WC Partition: Eurodoor, Schaefer
Dust Proof Paint: Desax, GA36 Gini
Pascal + Martine Varlet, PSS Interservice
Central Stockage Cleaning: Sonderegger P
WC Sink Counter/Mirror Cabinet:
Talsee, Kitchen: Läng Schreinerei und
Küchenbau
Door Stoppers: Phos Design
Interior Shading: Maison du Store
Exterior Gutter: Hirt

Cité du Temps:
Project Manager: Hayek Engineering AG
Site Supervision and Construction
Management: Itten+Brechbühl AG |
Sergio Gil López, Feim Hoti
Wood: Blumer-Lehmann
Concrete: Marti + Frutiger
HVAC: Engie Services, AGI
Sanitary: Engie Services, Oeschger
Brandschutz
Electricity: Etavis Jag Jakob, Fischer
Electric, Engie Services, ISP und Partner,
Siemens Schweiz, Dormakaba Schweiz,
PKE Elektronics
Façade: Sottas (curtainwall), MBM
Konstruktionen (conference hall

window), Roschmann(conference hall
roof)
Roof: S+T fassaden, BernaRoof,
Metallisten
PV Panel: Helion Solar
Metal Work: Metallbau von Arx
Elevator: EMCH Aufzüge
Ceiling System: KST
Dry Wall: Merz Gips
Plaster: B&L Bodensysteme
Terrazzo/Resin Floor: WALO
Bertschinger
Raised Floor: AGB Bautechnik
Parquet Floor: Intertapis
Interior Glass Wall System: BlessArt
Raumsysteme
Interior Wood Finish Wall/WoodDoor/
Reception Counter: Röthlisberger
Innenausbau
Tile: Blatter
Marble Stone: Schär + Trojahn
Bathroom Partition: Eurodoor
Bathroom Fitting: Talsee
Balustrade: MLG Metall und Planung
(glass), Charles Sauter (metal)
Retractable Staircase: HEMtech
Audio/Visual: Kilchenman, Swiss Timing
Conference Hall Furniture: Vifian
Möbelwerkstätte
Reception Lighting/Acoustic Unit:
Bestlight
Anti-graffiti Paint: Desax
Landscape: Hirt, Schwab Gartenbau,
Jacot des Combes, Bachofer, Wedatronic

Swatch Headquarters:
Project Manager: Hayek Engineering AG
Site Supervision and Construction
Management: Itten+Brechbühl AG
Wood: Blumer-Lehmann
Concrete: Marti + Frutiger
HVAC: Lippuner, Stoffel
Sanitary: Bären Haustechnik, Oeschger
Electrical: Etavis
Façade: Roschmann (roof), MBM
Konstruktionen (glass façade)
Glass Shutter: Bothe-Hild
Metal Work: Stauffer Metalbau, Herren
Metalbau, Hoffman Weibel, Adunic
Elevator: AS Aufzüge, EMCH
Ceiling System: KST, Creadec
Dry Wall: Nussbaum
Double Floor: AGB
Resin Floor: Nocita
Interior Glass Wall System: Glas Trösch
Wood Door: RWD Schlatter
Metal Door:
Tile: Blatter
WC Partition: Saka
WC Fitting: Talsee
Landsdcape: Herrmann Gartenbau,
Sutter Bauunternehmung, Hans Schmid,
Jacot des Combes, Hirt

Photographers:

Didier Boy de la Tour, Philipp Zinniker,
Nicolas Grosmond, Shigeru Ban
Architects Europe

Shigeru Ban

1957
Born in Tokyo

1977–80
Southern California Institute of
Architecture (SCI-Arc)

1980–82
The Cooper Union School of
Architecture

1982–83
Worked for Arata Isozaki, Tokyo, Japan

1984
Received Bachelor of Architecture from
The Cooper Union

1985
Established private practice in Tokyo

1993–95
Adjunct Professor of Architecture at
Tama Art University

1995–
Established NGO, Voluntary Architects
Network (VAN)

1995–99
Adjunct Professor of Architecture at
Yokohama National University
Consultant of United Nations High
Commissioner for Refugees (UNHCR)

1996–00
Adjunct Professor of Architecture at
Nihon University

2000
The Augustus Saint-Gaudens Award
from The Cooper Union, NY, USA

2000–01
Visiting Professor at Columbia University
Visiting Fellow of Donald Keen Center,
Columbia University

2001
Gengo Matsui Award

2001–
Member of Japan Institute of Architects
Member of Architectural Institute of
Japan

2001–08
Professor at Keio University

2004
Honorary Fellow of the American
Institute of Architects (HFAIA)
Grande Médaille d'Or, Prix de l'Académie
d'Architecture de France

2005
Thomas Jefferson Medalist in
Architecture
Arnold W. Brunner Memorial Prize in
Architecture
International Fellowship of the Royal
Institute of British Architects (IFRIBA)
Honorary Doctor of Humane Letters
Amherst College

2006
Honorary Fellow of the Royal
Architectural Institute of Canada
(HRAIC)

2006–09
Jury of Pritzker Architecture Prize

2008
Ordre National du Mérite, France (le
grade d'officier)

2009
Honorary Doctorate of Technical
University of Munich

2010
Visiting Professor at Harvard University
GSD
Visiting Professor at Cornell University
Ordre des Arts et des Lettres, France (le
grade d'officier)

2011–
Professor at Kyoto University of Art and
Design

2011
Auguste Perret Prize

2012
Mainichi Art Prize
Art Prize from Japanese Agency for
Cultural Affairs
Kalmanani Prize (Mexico City)

2014
Pritzker Architecture Prize
Honorary Doctorate from Cooper Union
Honorary Member of the Japan Institute
of Architects
Ordre des Arts et des Lettres, France (le
grade de commandeur)
Asia Game Changers Awards (Asia
Society, NY)
Joie de Vivre Award
Kyoto City Artistic and Cultural
Commendations, Sparkle Grand Award

2015
The Asahi Prize
Crystal Award (World Economic Forum,
Davos, Switzerland)
The Shigemitsu Award for Global
Cultural Exchange
Posey Leadership Award

2015–19
Guest Professor at Keio University

2017
Schweighofer Prize
Medal with Purple Ribbon
Mother Teresa Social Justice Award

2018
Golden Seat Master Award (China
Interior Design Week, Shanghai)

2019
Honorary Citizen of Tainan City, Taiwan
Yomiuri International Cooperation Prize

2019–
Professor at Keio University

REGISTRATION

First-Class Architect in Japan
Registered Architect in the States of
New York and Kentucky

Awards

1985

S. D. Review '85

1986

Design Competition for the redevelopment of Shinsaibashi, Osaka
Display of the Year Japan for "Emilio Ambasz" Exhibition

1988

Display of the Year Japan for "Alvar Aalto" Exhibition
Osaka Industrial Design Contest for L Unit System
S. D. Review '88

1989

Arflex Design Competition

1993

House Award, Tokyo Society of Architects

1995

Mainichi Design Prize for Paper Church

1996

Innovative Award, Tokyo Journal
Yoshioka Prize
JIA Kansai Architects for Paper Church
Ecoplice House Competition, IAA (International Architects Academy)

1997

The JIA Prize, Best Young Architect of the Year for Paper Church

1998

Tohoku Prize, Architectural Institute of Japan for Tazawako Station

1999

ar+d, Architectural Review, UK for Paper Church
4th International Festival for Architecture in Video by IMAGE, Italy
Architecture for Humanity Design Award for Paper Log House

2000

Akademie der Künste (Berlin Art Award) for Hannover Expo 2000 Japan Pavilion

2001

Nikkei New Office Award for GC Osaka Building
Time Magazine Innovator of the Year
World Architecture Awards 2001, Europe Category, Public/Cultural Category for the Japan Pavilion
The Prize of Japan Society Finishing Technology for GC Osaka Building

2002

World Architecture Awards 2002, Best House in the World for Naked House

2004

American Wood Design Award, Best of Non-residential for Atsushi Imai Memorial Gymnasium
AIA New York Chapter Design Awards, Project Honors for Nomadic Museum NY

2007

MIPIM Awards 2000, Residential Developments 1st Prize & Special Tribute for Kirinda House

2008

Urban Land Institute Awards for Excellence: Finalist for Kirinda House

2009

Japan Project International Award, Student Jury's Award: Chengdu Hualin Elementary School
AIJ Grand Prize for Nicolas G. Hayek Center

2010

International Architecture Awards, Grand Prize, for Haesley Nine Bridges Golf Clubhouse
International Award for Sustainable Architecture, Gold Medal for Haesley Nine Bridges Golf Clubhouse

2013

Elle Décor Design Award 2013, Wall Covering for Module H (Maison Hermès)
iF Design Award - lamp Yumi (floor lamp)

2014

Good Design Award for Yumi (floor lamp)

2015

ArchDaily Building of the Year 2015 Hospitality Architecture for Haesley Nine Bridges Golf Club House

2016

JIA Grand Prix 2015 for Oita Prefectural Art Museum
RIBA International Prize for International Excellence for Oita Prefecture Art Museum
Good Design Award 2016, Good Design Gold Award for Paper Partition System / Kumamoto Earthquake
AIA Awards - Architecture for Aspen Art Museum

2017

Good Design Award 2017, Good Design Special Award, Disaster Recovery Design for Wooden Prefabricated Temporary Housing / Kumamoto Earthquake

2018

JCD International Design Awards 2018 Grand Prize, Mt Fuji World Heritage Centre
Japan Wood Design Award 2018 for Mt Fuji World Heritage Centre

2019

2018 Wood Design & Building Awards, Merit Award for Shonai Hotel Suiden Terrasse

Publications

1997

shigeru ban, GG portfolio, Editorial Gustavo Gili, S.A., Spain

1998

JA30, SHIGERU BAN, The Japan Architect, Japan
Paper Tube Architecture from Kobe to Rewanda, Chikuma Shobo Publishing Co. Ltd., Japan

1999

SHIGERU BAN, Projects in Process, TOTO Publishing, Japan

2001

Shigeru Ban, Princeton Architectural Press, USA

2003

Shigeru Ban, Phaidon Press, New York/ London

2008

Shigeru Ban, Edilstampa, Italy

2009

Shigeru Ban, Paper in Architecture, Rizzoli, New York, USA

2010

Shigeru Ban. Complete Works 1985-2010, Taschen
Voluntary Architect' Network, INAX publication, Japan

2011

Shigeru Ban, Hachette Fascicoli

2012

Shigeru Ban, Taschen

2013

Shigeru Ban, NA Architects Series 07, Nikkei BP, Japan
How to make Houses. Shigeru Ban, Heibonsha, Japan

2014

Cardboard Cathedral, Auckland University Press, New Zealand
Humanitarian Architecture, Aspen Art Press/D.A.P., USA

2015

Shigeru Ban. Complete Works 1985-2015, Taschen

2016

Paper Tube Architecture, Iwanami, Japan
Shigeru Ban no Kenchiku Genba, Heibonsha, Japan

2017

Shigeru Ban - Material, Structure and Space, TOTO Publishing, Japan

2018

Shigeru Ban Architects, Images Publishing, USA
"纸建筑:建筑师能为社会做什么?", 天津凤凰空间文化传媒有限公司, China
"NA建筑家系列7-坂茂", 北京美术摄影出版社, China

2019

"행동하는 종이 건축", Minumsa, South Korea

Exhibitions

1984

Japanese Designer in New York, Gallery 91, New York, USA

1985

S. D. Review '85, Hillside Terrace Gallery, Tokyo
Adam in the Future, SEIBU Shibuya, Tokyo

1987

Tokyo Tower Project <40 Architects under 40>, Axis Gallery, Tokyo

1988

Models from Architect's Ateliers, Matsuya Gallery, Ginza, Tokyo
S.D. Review '88, Hillside Terrace Gallery, Tokyo

1989

Neo-Forma, Axis Gallery, Tokyo

1990

"KAGU" Exhibition, Makuhari messe
Last Decade 1990, Matsuya Gallery, Ginza, Tokyo
Virgin Collections, Guardian Garden

1993

Hardwares by Architects, Hanegi Museum, Tokyo
GA Japan League '93, GA Gallery, Tokyo
Chairs by Architects, Hanegi Museum, Tokyo

1994

Architecture of the Year '94, Metropolitan Plaza
GA Japan League '94, GA Gallery, Tokyo

1995

Paper Church and Volunteers, INAX Gallery, Osaka
Paper Church, Matsuya Gallery, Ginza, Tokyo
GA Japan League '95, GA Gallery, Tokyo

1996

Paper Church and Volunteers at Kobe, Kenchikuka Club, Aichi

1997

GA Japan League '97, GA Gallery, Tokyo
'97 JIA Prize for the Best Young Architect of the Year, Osaka, and Tokyo
Stool Exhibition 3, Living Design Center OZONE, Tokyo
Resurrection of Topos 3, Hillside Terrace Gallery, Tokyo

1998

GA Japan League '98, GA Gallery, Tokyo
'97 JIA Prize for the Best Young
Architect of the Year, Tokyo
GA Houses, GA Gallery, Tokyo

1999

Un-Private House, MoMA, New York,
USA
Cities on the Move, Hayward Gallery,
London, UK
Shigeru Ban, Ifa, France
Archi Lab, Orleans, France
Future Show, Bologna, Italy
Shigeru Ban, Projects in Process, Gallery
MA, Tokyo
GA Houses, GA Gallery, Tokyo
ArchiLab, Mori Art Museum Tokyo

2000

Japan Pavilion Hannover, Renate
Kammer Architektur und Kunst,
Hamburg, Germany
Venice Biennale, Paper Log House,
Venice, Italy
Paper Show by Takeo & Nippon Design
Center, Spiral Hall, Tokyo
Towards Total Space, Architecture
Museum, Netherlands

2001

Recent Projects, Zumtobel Light Forum,
Vienna, Austria
Recent Projects, Aedes East Forum,
Berlin, Germany

2002

GA Japan, Rietberg Museum
Competition, GA Gallery, Tokyo
Bamboo Roof, Rice University Art
Gallery, Houston, Texas, USA
Recent Projects, La Galerie
d'Architecture, Paris, France
Recent Projects, Arc en Rêve, Bordeaux,
France
2003 GA Houses 2003, Shutter House
for a Photographer, GA Gallery, Tokyo
Paper, Wood & Bamboo, Structural
Innovation in the Work of Shigeru Ban,
Harvard Design School, Cambridge,
Massachusetts, USA

2004

GA Houses, Villa Arno, GA Gallery,
Tokyo
New Trends of Architecture in Europe
and Japan, traveling exhibit-Europe and
Asia
Toward the Future: Museums by
Japanese Architects, traveling exhibit-
Japan
Venice Biennale, Centre Pompidou-
Metz, Venice, Italy
Paper Show by Takeo, Tokyo
Japan-Poland Exhibition, Poland
Arti & Architettura 1900-2000, Japan
Pavilion Hannover 2000, Palazzo

Ducale, Genoa, Italy
International Competition of
Architecture - Centre Pompidou-Metz -
The Six Projects of the World Museums
for a New Millennium, Centre Pompidou-
Metz Exhibition, traveling exhibit

2005

ArchiLab, New Experiments in
Architecture, Art and the City 1950-
2005, Tokyo

2006

Vasarely Pavilion, Aix-en-Provence,
France
Recent Projects, Faux Mouvement,
Metz, France

2007

Alvar Aalto Through the Eyes of Shigeru
Ban, Barbican, London, UK
Artek Pavilion, Milan, Italy
GA Houses, Dellis Cay Resort
Development West Beach Villa, GA
Gallery, Tokyo

2008

Japan Car Exhibition, Paris, London, UK
GA Houses, Picture Window House II,
GA Gallery, Tokyo, Japan
Shelter×Survival, Paper Log
House, Hiroshima City Museum of
Contemporary Art, Hiroshima
Davines, American Beauty Show,
Chicago, USA

2009

Frontiers of Architecture, Louisiana
Museum of Modern Art, Humlebæk,
Denmark
Dialogues for Emergency Architecture,
National Art Museum of China, Beijing,
China
Tokyo Fiber, Milan, Italy/Tokyo, Japan

2011

Irving Penn and Issey Miyake Exhibition,
21_21 design sight gallery, Tokyo
The World of Shigeru Ban Exhibition,
Hyogo

2012

Japan Foundation Architecture
Exhibition, Sendai, Japan/Paris, France
Architecture for Dogs (Paper Papillon),
Miami, USA

2013

House Vision 2013 Tokyo Exhibition,
Tokyo
Shigeru Ban, Architecture and
Humanitarian Activities, Art Tower Mito,
Mito
The Humanitarian Adventure: Reducing
Natural Risks, Red Cross Museum,
Geneva, Switzerland

Architecture for Dogs (Paper Papillon),
Gallery Ma, Tokyo

2014

Shigeru Ban: Humanitarian Architecture,
Aspen Art Museum, Colorado, USA
JP-CH 2014: Building in Context—
Contemporary Japanese Architecture
in Switzerland, Aoyama Spiral Garden,
Tokyo
Japan Architects 1945-2010, 21st
Century Museum of Contemporary Art,
Kanazawa
Architecture Since 3.11, 21st Century
Museum of Contemporary Art,
Kanazawa
Pierre Paulin – Design Forever, Channel
Nexus Hall, Tokyo

2015

The British Museum Exhibition: A
History of the World in 100 Objects,
Tokyo
Shigeru Ban – Paper Tube Structures
and Disaster Relief Projects, Lifestyle
Design Center, Tokyo
Reverberation: Pavilion of Light and
Sound - Clé de Peau Shiseido, Venice,
Italy

2016

Venivìce Biennale, Dreaming of Earth,
Venice, Italy
Sublime. Les tremblements du monde,
Paper Log House Kobe, Centre
Pompidou-Metz, Metz, France

2017

The Inventive Work of Shigeru Ban,
SCAF, Sydney, Australia
Japon, l'archipel de la maison, Hanegi
Forest Annex, Cité de l'architecture &
du patrimoine, Panasonic Shiodome
Museum, Tokyo
Shigeru Ban: Projects in Progress, TOTO
Gallery MA, Tokyo

2018

Japan in Architecture, Mori Museum,
Tokyo
Offsite: Shigeru Ban, Vancouver Art
Gallery, Canada
Bamboo Pavilion at Tongji University,
Shanghai, China

2019

GA International 2019, GA Gallery, Tokyo

2020

Beyond Japan, Yoshiro and Yoshio
Taniguchi Museum of Architecture,
Kanazawa
Shigeru Ban, Oita Prefectural Art
Museum, Oita

The architect
Shigeru Ban
visiting the
Swatch/Omega
Campus with
Philip Jodidio,
the author of this
book, July 29,
2019.

Photo Credits

Cover: © Swatch
p. 4: REUTERS/Benoit Tessier
p. 6: © Swatch
p. 9: © Omega
p. 10 (top): © Nicolas Grosmond
p. 10 (bottom): © Shigeru Ban Architects
pp. 14–15: © Shigeru Ban Architects
p. 16 (left): © Shigeru Ban Architects
p. 16 (right): © Shigeru Ban Architects
p. 19: © The Hyatt Foundation/Pritzker Architecture Prize
p. 20: © Swatch
p. 23: © Yukio Shimizu
p. 25: © Shigeru Ban Architects
p. 26: above: © Swatch; below: © Omega
p. 29: © Shigeru Ban Architects
p. 31: © Swatch Group
p. 32: Photo: © Hiroyuki Hirai
p. 34: © Yukio Shimizu
p. 35: Photographer: © Hiroyuki Hirai
p. 36: Photographer: © Hiroyuki Hirai
p. 37 (top): © Hiroyuki Hirai
p. 37 (bottom): © Hiroyuki Hirai
p. 38: © Didier Boy de la Tour
p. 39: © Didier Boy de la Tour
p. 40: Photo: © Hiroyuki Hirai
p. 41: © Didier Boy de la Tour
p. 42: © Air Images Philippe Guignard
p. 43 (left): © Didier Boy de la Tour
p. 43 (right): © Didier Boy de la Tour
p. 44: © Swatch
p. 47: © Blumer Lehmann ag
p. 48: © Swatch
p. 51: © Shigeru Ban Architects
p. 52: © Shigeru Ban Architects
p. 53: © Shigeru Ban Architects
p. 54: © Blumer Lehmann ag
p. 56: © Shigeru Ban Architects
p. 57: © Shigeru Ban Architects
pp. 58–59: © Shigeru Ban Architects
p. 60: © Shigeru Ban Architects
p. 61: © Shigeru Ban Architects
p. 62: © Shigeru Ban Architects
p. 63: © Philipp Zinniker / IttenBrechbühl
pp. 64–65: © Philipp Zinniker / IttenBrechbühl
p. 66 (top): © Blumer Lehmann ag
p. 66 (bottom): © Philipp Zinniker / IttenBrechbühl
p. 67: © Blumer Lehmann ag
p. 68: © Philipp Zinniker / IttenBrechbühl
p. 69: © Blumer Lehmann ag
p. 70: © Blumer Lehmann ag
p. 71: © Blumer Lehmann ag
pp. 72–73: © Swatch
pp. 74–75: © Swatch
p. 76: © Swatch
p. 77: © Swatch
p. 78: © Swatch
p. 79: © Didier Boy de la Tour
pp. 80–81: © Didier Boy de la Tour
p. 82: © Swatch
p. 83: © Swatch

p. 84: © Swatch
p. 85: © Swatch
pp. 86–87: © Swatch
p. 88 (top): © Swatch
p. 88 (bottom): © Didier Boy de la Tour
p. 89: © Didier Boy de la Tour
pp. 90–91: © Didier Boy de la Tour
p. 92 (top): © Swatch
p. 92 (bottom): © Swatch
p. 93: © Swatch
pp. 94–95: © Didier Boy de la Tour
p. 96: © Swatch
p. 97: © Swatch
p. 98: © Didier Boy de la Tour
p. 101: © Didier Boy de la Tour
p. 102: © Shigeru Ban Architects
p. 105 (top): © Shigeru Ban Architects
p. 105 (bottom): © Shigeru Ban Architects
p. 106: © Swatch Group
p. 108: © Shigeru Ban Architects
p. 109 (top): © SJB Kempter Fitze
p. 109 (bottom): © SJB Kempter Fitze
p. 110: © Shigeru Ban Architects
p. 111: Shigeru Ban Architects
p. 112: © Shigeru Ban Architects
p. 113: © Shigeru Ban Architects
p. 114: © Shigeru Ban Architects
p. 115: © Shigeru Ban Architects
p. 116: © Shigeru Ban Architects
p. 117: © Shigeru Ban Architects
pp. 118–119: Shigeru Ban Architects
p. 120: © Philip Zinniker for Blumer Lehmann ag
p. 121: © Shigeru Ban Architects
p. 122: © Shigeru Ban Architects
p. 123: © Shigeru Ban Architects
p. 124: © Shigeru Ban Architects
p. 125: © Shigeru Ban Architects
pp. 126–127: © Didier Boy de la Tour
pp. 128–129: © Swatch Group
pp. 130–131: © Swatch Group
p. 132: © Didier Boy de la Tour
p. 133: © Didier Boy de la Tour
p. 134: © Didier Boy de la Tour
p. 135: © Shigeru Ban Architects
pp. 136–137: © Didier Boy de la Tour
p. 138: © Didier Boy de la Tour
p. 139: © Didier Boy de la Tour
pp. 140–141: © Didier Boy de la Tour
pp. 142–143: © Didier Boy de la Tour
p. 144: © Didier Boy de la Tour
p. 145: © Didier Boy de la Tour
pp. 146–147: © Didier Boy de la Tour
pp. 148–149: © Swatch Group
p. 150: © Didier Boy de la Tour
p. 153: © Didier Boy de la Tour
pp. 154–155: © Didier Boy de la Tour
p. 157: © Didier Boy de la Tour
p. 160: © Shigeru Ban Architects
p. 161: © Shigeru Ban Architects
p. 162: © Shigeru Ban Architects
p. 163: © Shigeru Ban Architects
p. 164: © Shigeru Ban Architects
p. 165: © Shigeru Ban Architects
p. 166: © Shigeru Ban Architects
p. 167: © Shigeru Ban Architects
pp. 168–169: © Shigeru Ban Architects
pp. 170–171: © Philipp Zinniker /

IttenBrechbühl
p. 172 (top): © Shigeru Ban Architects
p. 172 (bottom): © Shigeru Ban Architects
p. 173: © Shigeru Ban Architects
pp. 174–175: © Philipp Zinniker / IttenBrechbühl
p. 176: © Shigeru Ban Architects
p. 177: © Philipp Zinniker / IttenBrechbühl
pp. 178–179: © Didier Boy de la Tour
pp. 180–181: © Didier Boy de la Tour
p. 182: © Didier Boy de la Tour
p. 183: © Didier Boy de la Tour
pp. 184–185: © Omega
p. 186: © Shigeru Ban Architects
p. 187 (top): © Omega
p. 187 (bottom): © Shigeru Ban Architects
p. 188: © Omega
p. 189: © Omega
pp. 190–191: © Didier Boy de la Tour
p. 192: © Didier Boy de la Tour
p. 193: © Omega
p. 194: © Didier Boy de la Tour
p. 195: © Didier Boy de la Tour
p. 196: © Omega
p. 197: © Omega
pp. 198–199: © Didier Boy de la Tour
p. 206 : © Didier Boy de la Tour

The author would like to thank Taro Okabe for his constant attention
to this project.

© Prestel Verlag, Munich · London · New York 2021
A member of Penguin Random House Verlagsgruppe GmbH
Neumarkter Strasse 28 · 81673 Munich

In respect to links in the book, Penguin Random House Verlagsgruppe
expressly notes that no illegal content was discernible on the linked sites at
the time the links were created. The Publisher has no influence at all over
the current and future design, content or authorship of the linked sites. For
this reason Penguin Random House Verlagsgruppe expressly disassociates
itself from all content on linked sites that has been altered since the link
was created and assumes no liability for such content.

A CIP catalogue record for this book is available from the British Library.

Editorial direction Prestel: Markus Eisen
Copyediting: Harriet Graham
Design and layout: Lou Benesch and Pablo de Gastines
Production management: Corinna Pickart
Separations: Reproline mediateam GmbH, Munich
Printing and binding: Grafisches Centrum Cuno GmbH & Co. KG, Calbe,
Germany
Typeface: Decimal
Paper: 150 g/m² Gardamatt Ultra

Penguin Random House Verlagsgruppe FSC® N001967

Printed in Germany

978-3-7913-7840-4

www.prestel.com